Bear Grylls

SURVIVAL SKILLS

HANDBOOK

VOLUME 1

CAMPING

•

MAPS & NAVIGATION

•

KNOTS

•

DANGERS & EMERGENCIES

CONTENTS

KNOTS

DANGERS AND EMERGENCIES

INTRODUCTION

We live on the most amazing planet, and should seize every chance we get to explore it. From the hottest desert to the highest mountain, I have been on lots of exciting adventures around the world, and seen some phenomenal parts of our planet. When you're out exploring, it's important to be prepared and to stay safe in the wild. Make sure you know about the area you are planning to go to beforehand – what is the weather like? What dangers are you likely to face? Once you know as much as you can, you will need to decide what equipment to take. It is very important to plan for emergency situations. When you're out in the wild, good preparation can be the difference between life and death. It is also vital that you are respectful of the world around us, and leave everything just as you found it. Exploring the world is a great privilege, and it is our responsibility to take care of our beautiful planet so we can continue adventuring for many years to come.

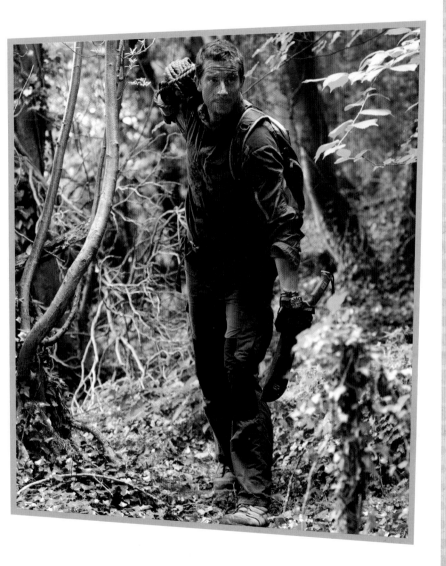

CAMPING

Camping in the great outdoors can be one of the most rewarding experiences – as long as you are fully prepared for a night under the stars. Once you know how to build a campfire, safely store food, and build your shelter you can embark on great adventures!

Bear

IN THIS SECTION:

GOING CAMPING!

Camping with friends and family can be a mini-adventure! A good campsite will allow you to enjoy your surroundings and should be kind to the environment. You should also be able to relax there safely. Take the time to fully prepare for your trip and you'll make great memories in the outdoors.

Making camp

Camp at existing campsites when possible, and remember that good campsites are found, not made.

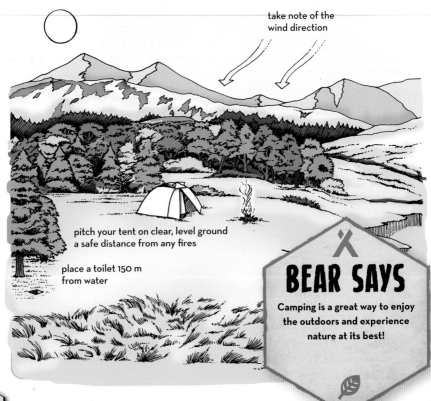

take note of the wind direction

pitch your tent on clear, level ground a safe distance from any fires

place a toilet 150 m from water

BEAR SAYS

Camping is a great way to enjoy the outdoors and experience nature at its best!

Places to avoid
Some locations are not good for camping – stay away at all costs!

Flood risk
Washouts, gullies, and floodplains can be deadly when it rains.

Under a tree
Even healthy-looking branches may drop without warning.

Cliff base
Don't camp below a cliff or a steep rocky slope in case loose rocks fall.

Avalanche risk
Stay away from steep slopes during or after heavy snowfall.

TENTS

A tent is your home away from home while camping. It shelters you from wind, rain, cold temperatures, and blazing Sun. There are lots of different types to choose from.

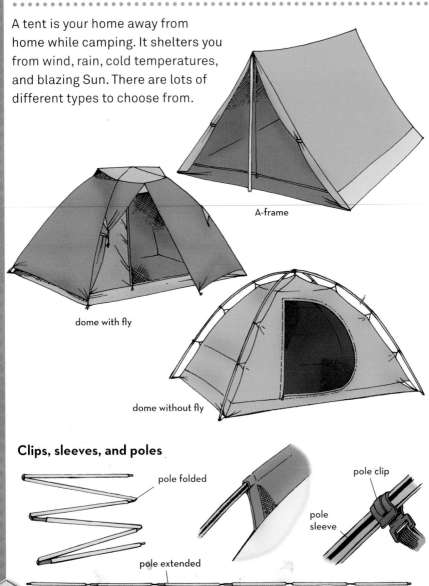

A-frame

dome with fly

dome without fly

Clips, sleeves, and poles

pole folded

pole extended

pole sleeve

pole clip

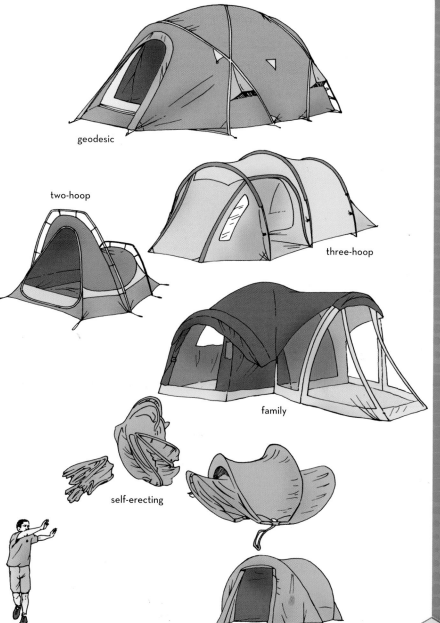

geodesic

two-hoop

three-hoop

family

self-erecting

Pegs

Very few tents will stay up by themselves, and, even then, only in good weather. They need guy ropes (ropes under tension) and secure attachments to the ground. That's where pegs come in.

peg puller

steel

aluminium

plastic

mallet and extractor

wooden stake

plastic twist

glow-in-the-dark

aluminium sand

plastic sand

delta

ancient Roman

sand anchor

standard

Placing pegs

It is important to make sure your tent is stable and stays put so that you have proper shelter.

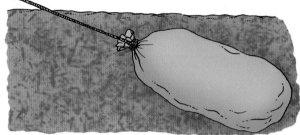

Mountain favourite

A buried sleeping bag case filled with snow makes a good anchor.

Standard

The rope is at 90° to the peg.

Super stable

When stability is key, use two pegs for extra security.

Delta

These strong pegs keep a very secure hold.

Back-up

Use a heavy rock to secure a peg if it won't go far into the ground.

Rocks

Piles of rocks can be used to anchor your lines.

Ice

A tent peg can be placed in a hole in the ice.

Desert sand

A peg buried in sand makes a good anchor.

Buried in ice

A peg can be frozen in ice to secure its hold.

Parachute

Place heavy objects in a parachute anchor, then bury.

What to do if your tent leaks

If you expect wet weather or a downpour looms, these simple tips can save the day.

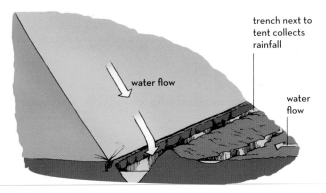

Water trench

A bit of digging can help avoid a flood in your tent.

water flow

trench next to tent collects rainfall

water flow

Inside drip string

This short-term fix allows leaking water to drip into a bowl rather than your sleeping bag.

string

stone

Outside string

This diverts water from reaching the anchor point of your tent or tarp.

Duct tape

Apply to a hole or split seam.

Hole patch

Patch kits will securely seal a leaking hole.

Seam sealer

Use a sealer for leaks along the seam.

OTHER TYPES OF SHELTER

From tarpaulin to igloos, there are many other types of shelter that could be a better option than a tent.

The art of tarp
These are some ways tarpaulin can be made into a shelter.

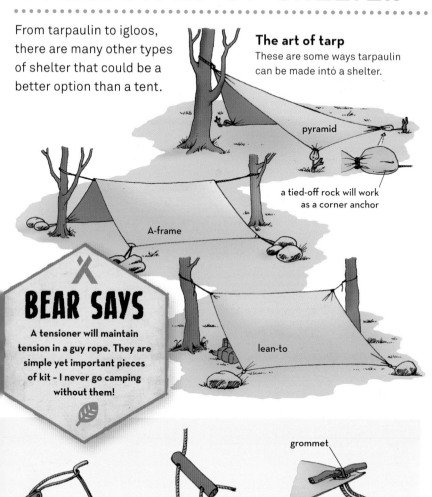

pyramid

a tied-off rock will work as a corner anchor

A-frame

lean-to

BEAR SAYS

A tensioner will maintain tension in a guy rope. They are simple yet important pieces of kit – I never go camping without them!

Plastic line
A small tug on this tensioner will tighten the guy ropes.

Timber line
A piece of timber with two holes will also hold guy ropes in place.

grommet

Stick anchor
This simple method will save wear on your tarp corner grommets.

bivouac bags, also known as "bivvy" bags, are cheaper and lighter alternatives to tents

camping hammock

Mongolian yurt

American Indian Great Plains teepee

Snow cave

With experience and a snow shovel, you and a friend can build a comfortable snow cave in a couple of hours. They can be a life-saver, but you have to be careful of carbon monoxide gas poisoning.

ventilation hole

skis or other equipment can alert your position to others

Igloo

This Inuit invention is an option for shelter in cold conditions.

BEAR SAYS

Snow is a great insulator in freezing conditions. Once you have made your shelter, compress snow into blocks to seal up the entrance.

How to make an igloo

1 Mark a circle in the snow about 2 m across.

2 Tramp down the snow inside the circle until you have a solid surface.

1. To make a snow block, first cut two parallel lines

snow saw

3. Lastly, make a vertical cut

2. Then make horizontal cut

3 Using a snow saw, cut blocks of hard, compacted snow. Hard snow can usually be found below soft snow.

5 Cut a ramp in the snow blocks halfway around the circle.

4 Arrange your first blocks in a circle.

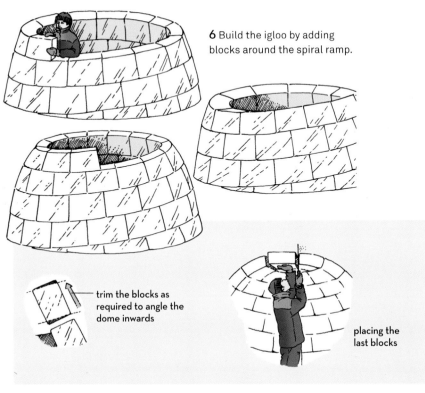

6 Build the igloo by adding blocks around the spiral ramp.

trim the blocks as required to angle the dome inwards

placing the last blocks

7 Dig an entrance underneath the igloo.

8 Build an entrance roof from two slabs of snow.

How to make a quinzee

A quinzee is a large pile of snow that has been hollowed out.

1 Put backpacks and any other bulky gear together.

2 Pile up a good-sized amount of snow over your backpacks.

3 Pack down the snow and wait a couple of hours while it "sinters" (this is when the snow crystals bind to each other).

4 Stick even-lengthed sticks all around the snow pile.

5 Excavate the snow. The other ends of the sticks will guide you and keep you from digging through.

air hole

6 Insulate the base with tarps or sleeping mats, and make yourself at home.

SLEEPING SOFTLY

A camping mattress makes sleeping more comfortable, and also keeps you warmer than if you were to sleep directly on the ground.

foam mat

foam mat with elastic straps

self-inflating open cell foam

double air mattress

single air mattress with air pillow

Pumps

electric pump

hand pump

foot pump (uses bellows)

SLEEPING BAGS

A good-quality sleeping bag is essential for a good night's sleep in the outdoors.

🏕

BEAR SAYS

Sleeping bags are such an important piece of kit! You'll want to make sure you have the right type depending on the temperature at night.

rectangular

mummy sleeping bag with hood

double sleeping bag

22

compression sack

stuff bag

Sleeping bag fillings

A sleeping bag is made up of a lining and an outer shell. In between the two are different types of filling. The way in which the filling is stitched together affects how warm you stay inside it. Down bags are often built with pockets called baffles that stop the down from bunching.

sewn through – outer shell is stitched together

offset quilt – staggered double layers

shingles – layered like roof tiles

box-shaped baffle

slant box baffle

trapezoidal baffle

V-tube baffle

KNIVES

A good sharp knife is a camping essential but should only be used by an adult with caution and care.

Leatherman multi-tool

Opinel folding knife

knife with leather sheath

parang

Survival knife

sharpening stone

sheath

wire saw

handle cap compass

fishing line, hooks, and sinkers

matches and striker

hollow handle

blade

Scout knife

Swiss Army knife

folding knife

BEAR SAYS

Knives can have fixed or folding blades, and often come with other tools too.

Parts of a hunting knife

blade

thumb grip

hilt

rivets

spacer

handle

tang

rivet hole

the assembled knife

Knife sharpening

To sharpen a knife, the blade is often passed over a hard, rough surface.

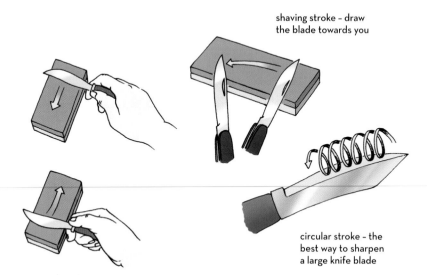

shaving stroke – draw the blade towards you

circular stroke – the best way to sharpen a large knife blade

figure eight stroke – draw the blade back and forth

Useful tools

Chop
Only large blades should be used for chopping.

Whittle
Use a small knife for fine carving.

Carve
To carve, make shallow cuts along the grain.

honing oil

honing stone

sharpening tool

sharpening steel

BEAR SAYS

Knives are very useful pieces of equipment and they require a lot of special care.

10 degrees
For light duty and fine work such as filleting and shaving. The edge will blunt fairly quickly.

20 degrees
A good angle for everyday use. To approximate it, imagine half of 90 degrees, then half of 45 degrees.

30 degrees
A somewhat blunt yet long-lasting edge for heavy-duty work, such as chopping wood.

TOILETS AND SHOWERS

For a healthy environment and a healthy you, make sure you maintain hygiene by washing and showering. Depending on your needs, there are different types of toilet that can be built outdoors.

Cat hole
For one-time, personal use.

Long-stay latrine

wicker privacy screen

safety string

urinal

soil

stones

plastic or bark funnel

stockpile of soil

Latrine for a large group

Keeping clean

soap

hand wash

antibacterial wipes

Using a solar shower

1 Fill the shower bag with water and lay it in the sun. On a cool or overcast day, do this in the morning so that there is warm water in the afternoon.

2 Hang the bag from a tree. The bag will be heavy, so pick a branch that is strong and healthy.

BEAR SAYS

Staying clean may not always be an obvious part of survival – but without it hygiene will suffer, making infections more likely.

3 Check that the water is at a safe temperature before starting your shower.

you could hang a curtain for privacy

FOOD CACHES

You don't want to share your precious food supplies with the local wildlife. In some places hungry bears may look for a meal.

Bear caches

Traditional cache
These mini log cabins are raised up high off the ground. They are still used in North American woods

removable ladder

Camping ground cache
These permanent bear-proof cabinets are a common sight in camping grounds where bears might visit.

Bear can
These tough canisters can hold about a week's worth of food for the average hiker.

Setting up a throwline bear cache

1 Find two trees about 4.5 m apart. Throw the rope up and over a branch.

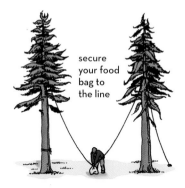

secure your food bag to the line

2 Tie the rope to the tree trunk then throw the rope over a branch on the second tree.

3 Then, hoist it up until it's at least 3.5 m above the ground.

4 Tie the other end of the line to the trunk of the second tree. Your food is now safe.

✗
BEAR SAYS

Bears have an incredible sense of smell, and are also able to recognize the sight of food containers.

NUTRITION

Eating well is the key to good health. This is especially true if you are getting active outdoors. Make sure you get a balanced intake of water, various food groups, vitamins, and minerals.

Water

The most vital substance in our bodies is water. It makes up more than half of a person's bodyweight, and fulfils such important roles that even a few days without it can be fatal.

BEAR SAYS

On days when you are active you will need more food and water than usual. Always stay hydrated – especially in hot weather.

Micronutrients

Micronutrients are essential vitamins and minerals that are needed in very small quantities for different body functions. Examples include salt and the vitamins and minerals found in leafy vegetables, fruit, and vitamin supplements.

Carbohydrates

Carbohydrates are the body's prime energy source. They are found in bread, pasta, rice, potatoes, fruit, and sweets.

Fats

Fats are essential for processing some vitamins, promoting healthy cell function, and are a rich source of energy.

Protein

Protein builds up, maintains, and replaces body tissues. It is essential for muscle growth and a healthy immune system.

Healthy eating

This is a graphic guide to a healthy meal. You should have more fruit and vegetables than any other food group. Cut down on big portion sizes, extra fats, and foods that are high in sugar and salt.

fats and sweets
(eat sparingly)

meat, poultry, fish, and nuts

milk, yogurt, and cheese

vegetables

fruit

bread, cereal, rice, and pasta
(include with most meals)

FOOD FOR THE OUTDOORS

A healthy diet is essential when you are enjoying the outdoors. When planning a trip, choose food that is healthy, tasty, lightweight, and doesn't need to be kept cold.

Hiking fuel

If you're on a big hike, your body will need a lot more food than normal. Graze on these easily digested, energy-rich foods to keep you going for hours.

trail mix – nuts, dried fruit, sultanas, raisins, and seeds

biscuits

chocolate

crackers

cereal bar

sweets

Breakfast

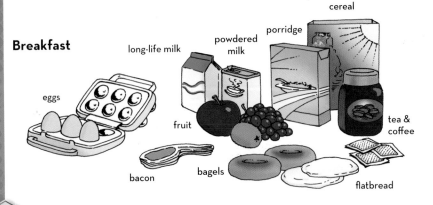

cereal

porridge

powdered milk

long-life milk

eggs

fruit

tea & coffee

bacon

bagels

flatbread

Lunch

bread
cheese
salami
powdered fruit drink
crackers
sardines
fruitcake
fruit
jam
salad and vegetables

Dinner

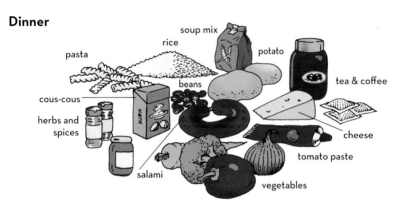

soup mix
rice
pasta
potato
beans
tea & coffee
cous-cous
herbs and spices
cheese
tomato paste
salami
vegetables

Dessert

scone or muffin
chocolate
hot chocolate
apple or apricot crumble with custard
toasted marshmallow

FIRE MAKING

Humans have been making and cooking on campfires for a few hundred thousand years. Making fire is still an important skill to so that you can keep warm and cook when camping.

Fire triangle

There are three elements that must be present for a fire to exist: oxygen, fuel, and heat. You'll need them in the right combination to get your fire started. Removing one or more of these elements will put out the fire.

Tinder

Tinder is a fine flammable material that easily catches a spark.

Bark
Look for dry inner bark from dead logs.

Moss
Dead, dry moss makes an excellent fire starter.

Grass
Break down stalks of dry grass into fine fibres.

Fungus
The inner flesh from bracket fungus is flammable.

Cotton wool and petroleum jelly
A highly flammable mix.

Leaves
Dry dead leaves are often easy to find.

Parts of a fire

tinder

kindling

small fuel

main fuel

large fuel

Build it up

A good fire is built up gradually. Start with tinder, then once the tinder has begun to burn, add kindling – dry twigs and sticks no thicker than your little finger. As coals are created, slowly add larger pieces of fuel.

Starting structures

tepee

lean-to

log cabin

A-frame

FIRE STARTING

Starting fires has been a straightforward task ever since the invention of matches and lighters. However, there are other ways to create a spark if you don't have these tools available.

BEAR SAYS

Flint can be used to start fires even when wet, making it an incredibly useful piece of kit.

Heat sources

lighter

matches

focused sunlight will ignite tinder

magnifying glass

soft-drink can

carbon
steel blade

ferrocerium
rod

chocolate

Parabolic can

Polish the base of a can with chocolate
or toothpaste until it is mirror smooth
and highly reflective (this may take
several hours).

Flint and steel

The "flint" component of a flint and
steel fire-starting kit is actually
made of a metal alloy called
ferrocerium. When struck with
steel, it gives out sparks.

Battery method

steel wool

nine-volt
battery

two AA
batteries

steel wool

Electric spark

When steel wool is brushed against the contacts of a
battery, it will glow brightly and begin to burn. A nine-
volt battery is most convenient for this method, but any
battery will work, including one from a mobile phone.

Magnesium fire block

These fire-starting kits consist of a steel striker and a block of magnesium with a ferrocerium rod fixed down one side. They are small and light, and are still effective in damp conditions.

steel striker

magnesium block

ferrocerium rod

1 To begin, use a knife blade to scrape a small pile of shavings from the magnesium block. The shavings are light, so protect the pile from the breeze.

2 Collect the shavings and gather them in a little nest of dry tinder.

3 Run the ferrocerium rod along the steel striker or a knife blade. The resulting sparks will catch in the magnesium shavings and burn a very intense, white-hot flame for a few seconds – long enough to get your tinder burning.

Hand drill

A hand drill consists of a softwood drill and fireboard. Run your hands down the drill as you spin it, to maintain pressure and build friction.

drill

fireboard

tinder

Fire piston

This ancient device is from Southeast Asia and the Pacific. Quickly pushing the piston into the cylinder causes a spark to be ignited in the tinder.

piston

cylinder

tinder is placed at the end of the piston

temperature 315°C

Fire plough

Cut a straight groove along a softwood base. Plough the tip of a hardwood rod back and forth along this groove. As friction builds up, small wood fibres will become detached from the groove. Eventually the detached fibres will start smoldering and form a "coal". Use this to ignite your tinder.

smoldering fibres

Bow drill

The bow drill is slightly more complicated than other friction fire-starting methods, but once mastered, it is extremely effective – even when temperatures are cool or weather conditions are humid.

spindle

bow

cord or leather thong

fireboard

tinder

notch cut in baseboard to hold tinder

Blowing tinder

The end result of many fire-starting methods is not a flame but a precious glowing ember. To really get the fire started, quickly gather the ember into a bundle of tinder and blow gently. This adds oxygen and raises the temperature enough for the material to burn.

Carrying fire

It can be easier to carry embers rather than to start a fire without matches or a lighter. To do this, punch a few holes in a can and attach a string or wire for a handle. Then place the embers between two layers of dry moss. Check the embers from time to time, and blow on them if they are starting to fade. Well cared for, the embers should last several days.

moss

embers

moss

COOKING WITH FIRE

As well as providing warmth and a place to gather, the main purpose of a campfire is to cook your food.

Stable fireplace
Use three stones to support the pot.

Natural skewers
Fish and meat can be grilled on sticks over the fire.

Handy branches
Using a support branch to control height, a forked branch can hold several utensils.

Wind assisted
The open side of a three-sided fireplace should face into the wind.

Basic construction
Put two logs parallel to the wind to form a simple fireplace.

An easy spit
Sharpened branches driven into the ground offer a sturdy spit.

Uneven surface
Use the slope of the ground and some large rocks to help support your utensils over the fire.

Longer term
If you are staying in one place for a while, dig a hole for a more permanent fireplace.

Star fire
Push in the logs as they burn to create a long-lasting cooking spot.

Crane
This arrangement will keep your cooking pot off the fire, and keep it from getting smothered.

Adjustable crane
This crane allows you to move your pot up and down so that you can control the temperature it is exposed to.

Stone griddle
A slab of stone will take a long time to heat, but will stay hot for a long time. Use a dry, solid rock.

Bamboo cooking pot

Green bamboo is very fire resistant and makes an excellent pot for boiling and simmering.

food goes here

steam

water

Bamboo steamer

Punch a few holes in each of the two walls that divide a length of bamboo into three sections. Put water in one end and food in the other and you have a steamer.

Breakfast in a bag

Line the bottom of a damp paper bag with bacon, then crack an egg on top. Place the bag on some hot coals and ashes to cook.

Foil oven

Wrap a whole meal in tinfoil and put it into the coals for a slow roast. By using this method exclusively, you can save on the weight of cooking pots and pans.

Hangi

The hangi is a traditional New Zealand Maori method of cooking large communal meals. To make a hangi, first dig a pit in the ground. Then build a pyre of wood beams over the pit to carry the hangi stones. Set the pyre ablaze to super-heat the stones. Once they have dropped into the pit, add the food in wire baskets, cover in damp sacks and soil, and leave to cook for two to three hours.

soil

damp burlap sacks

hot rocks

Mud baking

1 Gut a fish and lay it on a bed of non-poisonous green leaves. There is no need to remove the scales.

2 Fold the leaves over the fish, ensuring that it is completely covered. Bind the package with twine.

3 Pack mud all around the package. Use clay if it is available, or use mud that has a clay-like texture. Check for holes.

4 Bury the package in hot coals. A medium-sized fish should take about 20 minutes to cook.

CAMPING STOVES

Cooking meals on an open fire has its downsides. Things get sooty, and it can be hard to find fuel. Often, a camping stove is the best way to cook outdoors.

Fuel stoves

multi-fuel stove

double burner

butane/propane cartridge and burner attachment

single burner with butane canister

Alcohol burner set

pan

burner

pot

ready to cook

pot lifter

Primus paraffin stove

Invented in 1892, the Primus pressurized paraffin burner was the original camping and expedition stove.

US Army gasoline-burning stove

These stoves were standard US Army issue from 1951 until 1987.

Cooking without gas

Parabolic solar cooker

Solar cookers are the ultimate in environmentally friendly cooking. Parabolic cookers can reach high temperatures very quickly and are good for bringing liquids to a boil.

Twig stove

This low-impact twig burner can be easily made from a steel can and wire using basic tools.

BEAR SAYS

If you are prepared, cooking in the wild can be easy. Be extra careful with camping stoves, however, as they can reach extreme temperatures.

Solar box oven

This design makes use of reflective panels and a sealed light-absorbent chamber. Temperatures inside can reach 148°C.

MAPS AND NAVIGATION

Learning essential skills such as map reading and navigation will allow you to truly experience the world around you. Although it requires practice and practical application, there is nothing like the sense of achievement you will feel upon successfully finding your way to your planned destination!

IN THIS SECTION:

STARTING YOUR ADVENTURE

The world is full of exciting places to explore. In order to stay safe on your travels you will need to learn the art of navigation and map reading, like the adventurers of the past. As long as you have a map and compass, and know how to use them, you need never get lost. Remember, practice makes perfect!

Equipment

If you venture into the wild, make sure you have all the equipment you need so that you can get from one place to another as quickly and easily as possible. The type of equipment and the amount you need depends upon where you are going and for how long. Here are some of the basics you will need when going walking.

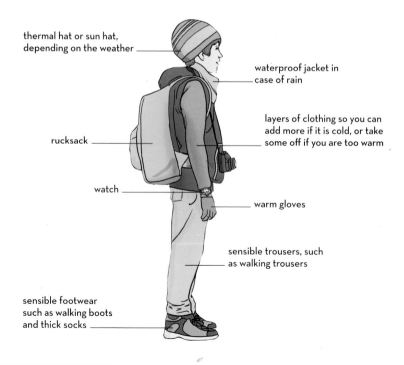

thermal hat or sun hat, depending on the weather

waterproof jacket in case of rain

layers of clothing so you can add more if it is cold, or take some off if you are too warm

rucksack

watch

warm gloves

sensible trousers, such as walking trousers

sensible footwear such as walking boots and thick socks

Make sure you carry these essentials in your rucksack or day bag.

compass

map

first-aid kit

food and bottle of water

torch

mobile phone

camera

sunscreen and insect repellant

emergency contact details

BEAR SAYS

Make sure someone knows your route and estimated arrival time before you set off so they can raise the alarm if you don't turn up when expected.

MAPS

Map care

As you walk, you will need to look at your map quite often to check you are on the right track. Maps need to be folded carefully to keep them in good condition so that they stay useful.

A map case with a neck cord may be a good idea, while some outdoor clothing has a specially designed large map pocket – if you are keeping the map in a bag, make sure it is easily accessible when you are out. Laminated maps can be useful if you are likely to be outside in wet or windy weather conditions. A spare may also be essential if you are somewhere remote.

How to fold a map

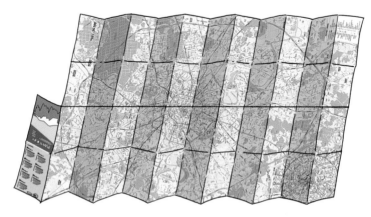

1 Although it sounds easy, folding a map can be tricky. With your map spread open, look at the creases – they should show the correct places to fold.

2 Fold the map in half by bringing the top edge to meet the bottom edge.

make sure the cover is out to one side

3 Fold the map inwards, as though it is an accordion.

4 Fold the map over so that the cover is on top. Some maps have a third section that needs to be tucked in.

BEAR SAYS

Explorers should be good at drawing maps, so it is important to get lots of practice. You never know when you might need these skills!

Topographical maps

These maps show contour lines and landforms. They are useful because they show how the ground is shaped. Every hiker should be able to "read" the contour lines on the map so that they can plan their route.

Contour lines

Each contour line on a map joins up points where the ground is the same height. Lines close together mean that there is a steep slope, while lines that are far apart indicate flat ground or a gentle slope.

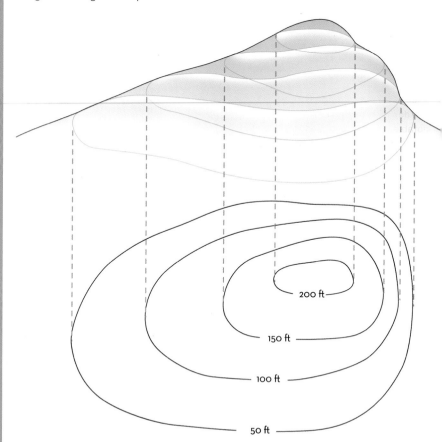

200 ft

150 ft

100 ft

50 ft

Choosing the best route

The best route to a destination may not be the most direct. Choose a path that is safe – for example on footpaths – and stay away from any hazards like cliffs and fast-moving water. Make it as simple as possible so that it is easy to follow and make sure you have permission to be on the land if it isn't a public right of way.

Landmark spotting

From your known start point, look for the nearest and biggest landmark on your map, such as a lake. Check the contour lines in case it is hidden from view. If you don't know where you are, mark any notable landmarks around you on a piece of paper and then see if you can match them up to your map. The scale may be tricky to guess but it is good start if you are unsure of your location.

BEAR SAYS

Understanding contour lines and being able to visualize your environment from a map is a great skill to have under your belt.

NORTH

WEST

EAST

SOUTH

How to measure distance

Map measurers allow you to find the distances between two points on a map. Route planning is an important part of navigation, and knowing how far you need to travel will help you work out your finish time – and if you'll arrive before dark!

map scale

needle

Analogue map reader

This tool uses a needle and dial printed with different map scales to show distance in miles or kilometres.

Using your compass

As well as taking bearings and helping you find north, your orienteering compass can help you find distances, using the measurements on the base plate.

display

input
buttons

wheel

Digital map reader

With digital map reader wheels, the user sets the unit, such as kilometres, and the map scale. They then run the tip of the reader along the route to find the distance.

BEAR SAYS

Measuring distance accurately will help you plan your hike. Take the time to take measurements before you set off.

Using a piece of string

If you are without a device, you can place a piece of string along your route, and then along the distance scale on the map.

Types of landscape

As you walk around the countryside you will notice that there are many different types of landscape. Some are far easier to travel along than others. These are some of the most common types.

Gentle slope
This slope decreases steadily in height and makes for an easy climb.

Steep slope
Steep slopes are hard to trek up, due to the sharp angle of the land.

Concave slope

This kind of slope is steep at the top but less so at the bottom, a little like the curve inside a bowl.

BEAR SAYS

Make sure you avoid steep climbs! A knowledge of contour lines will help you pick the best paths while navigating.

Convex slope

A rounded slope that goes from less steep to steep.

Cliff

A cliff is a very steep drop in the landscape, often at coasts.

Gullies and spurs

Gullies are steep ravines found close to the seashore, while spurs are the ridges of land that slope down from the edge of a hill.

Saddle
The area between two connecting hills or mountain peaks is called a saddle.

BEAR SAYS

A landscape is made up of different geographic features that can be used make navigation much easier.

Valley
A valley is a low area of land found between hills. Rivers are often found in valleys.

Symbols

Maps use symbols, lines, and colours to describe what is on the land and make the map clearer.

Learn the pictures

If you look closely at a map you can see it is covered in symbols. It would be almost impossible to write everything out in words on a map – there just isn't enough space. A key (or legend) explains what these symbols mean. The symbols could be pictures, words, or abbreviations.

A symbol for Mars

Ordnance Survey is the national mapping agency for Great Britain and is one of the world's largest producers of maps. The symbols used on these maps are easily recognizable and in May 2016 they held a competition to design a symbol for Mars as it has been recently mapped.

Campsite

Motorway

Railway

Railway station

River

Sch   School

Place of worship

P   Post office

Woods

Scales

Maps are made to scale so that the distance between landmarks and places in real life is shown accurately on paper. It is very important that the map is correct, so that features are where the map reader expects. Scale also helps us to work out distances. Most maps have a scale written on them (e.g. 1:50,000). This means that one centimetre on the map represents 50,000 cm on the ground.

Small scale

The scale is shown visually on a map in both centimetres and inches. In this example, this diagram shows a map with a scale of 1:100,000. In this case every one centimetre on the map is equal to one kilometre on the ground.

BEAR SAYS

Learning the symbols can take time at first but they are quite straightforward. Put the time in to make sure you recognize them now to make life easier.

Coordinates

Coordinates can describe any location on Earth. Our planet is a globe or sphere, and around it are a set of imaginary rings drawn from east to west and north to south. The lines running from the top to the bottom of the globe are called lines of longitude, while the lines running around it are called lines of latitude.

Lines of latitude

Latitude is measured in degrees north or south of the equator (0–90°). The equator is an imaginary line that runs round the centre of the planet, and is itself a line of latitude. It divides the Earth into two parts – the northern and southern hemispheres.

Lines of longitude

Lines of longitude run around the Earth from north to south. They are called meridians. Longitude is measured in degrees east or west of the Greenwich meridian (0–180°).

northern hemisphere

WEST

equator

SOUTH

BEAR SAYS

Using longitude and latitude you can accurately describe any location on Earth.

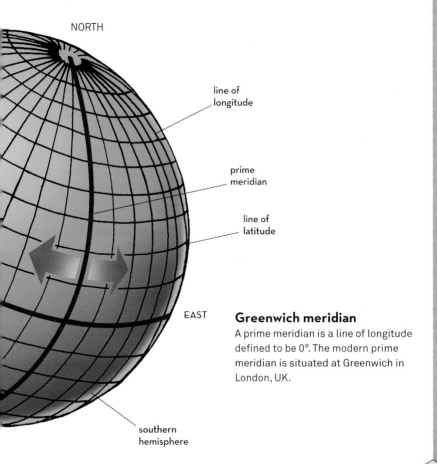

Where do you live?

The coordinate system can be used to pinpoint anywhere on the planet, and works in any language because it relies on numbers. You can look up the latitude and longitude of where you live on the internet.

NORTH

line of longitude

prime meridian

line of latitude

EAST

southern hemisphere

Greenwich meridian

A prime meridian is a line of longitude defined to be 0°. The modern prime meridian is situated at Greenwich in London, UK.

From globe to map

Our planet is a sphere – but maps are flat. In order to create a map, cartographers have to "project" the 3D globe onto 2D paper by squashing and stretching it. Luckily, the changes made to the globe are too small to cause big problems on most hiking maps.

EARTH

cylindrical projection

there are three main ways maps are projected onto flat paper

Grid references

Maps are often divided into squares called grids. These grids help to pinpoint a location on the map quickly. The vertical lines crossing the map from top to bottom are called "eastings" because the numbers go up as you move east across the map. The horizontal lines crossing the map from one side to the other are called "northings" as the numbers increase as you get further north.

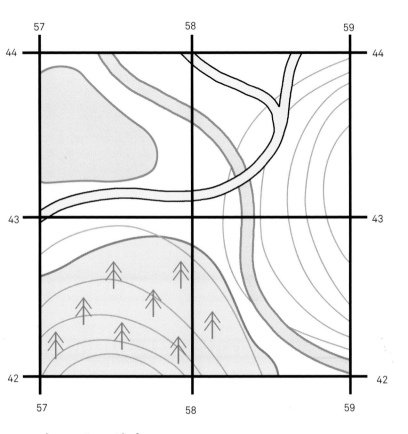

when you give a grid reference you always give the eastings first. The forest is in 5742.

MAGNETIC EARTH

Our planet is one big magnet, which is very useful for navigation – just as long as you have a map, a compass, and an understanding of how magnetic north and true north differ.

Earth's magnetic field

At Earth's centre is liquid iron. This metal core makes our planet into a giant magnet, with a magnetic field that changes over time. Because magnetic north is not at the geographic North Pole, you need to make special adjustments when using a compass. This is known as declination.

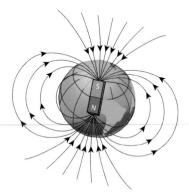

Earth's magnetic field is strongest near the North and South Poles.

Which way is north?

When we talk about "true north" we mean the top of Earth – the geographic North Pole. Earth spins around, and if you imagine it is spinning around a line that goes from the top to the bottom of the planet, the North Pole is the point at the very top, and the South Pole is the point at the very bottom. Magnetic north is different as it responds to Earth's changing magnetic field, and doesn't line up with the same point.

magnetic North Pole

geographic North Pole

11.5°

geographic South Pole

Three norths

Good maps will have a key to indicate grid, true (geographic), and magnetic north.

grid north

true north

magnetic north

BEAR SAYS

GPS systems are not affected by the earth's magnetic field, so they can be a useful piece of kit, especially in the far north.

COMPASSES

The compass was invented in China around a thousand years ago and it is still used today by navigators needing to find their direction of travel. It works using a tiny magnet controlled by Earth's magnetic field, which makes the compass point north.

Which compass should I use?

An orienteering compass is a great place to start. It has a transparent base and is designed to be used with a topographical map. It is is a very useful piece of kit and, with practice, is easy to use. No matter which way you turn, the magnetic needle always points north, so you can discover which way is north, east, south, and west.

scale

direction of travel arrow

magnifier

scale

scale

orienting arrow

magentic needle

orienting lines

dial

Orient a map

To orient a map you need to align the edge of your compass with the north–south lines of your map. Set the dial of your compass to north, then turn the map and compass together until the north (red) end of the compass needle is directly over the orienting arrow. Your map is now correctly oriented.

when the map is correctly oriented, a line drawn from your position on the map to a mapped landmark will point to the actual landmark

to true north

to true north

your location on map

Take a bearing

The angle between north and an object is called a bearing. They are measured in degrees, for example 45 degrees (45°). Bearings are always measured clockwise – you start facing north and turn to the right until you reach the angle of the bearing. Then you should be facing your destination. A bearing can also be known as a "magnetic" or "true" bearing depending upon whether it is measured from true north or magnetic north.

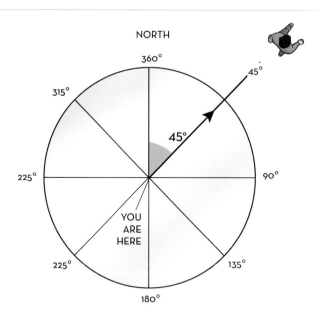

Try it yourself!

These diagrams show a hiker walking in three different directions. Can you work out his bearing for each picture?

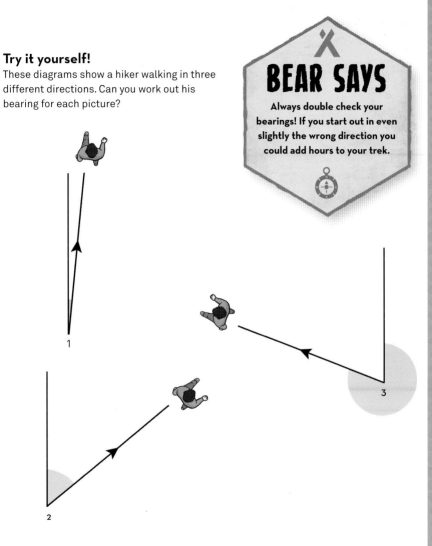

BEAR SAYS

Always double check your bearings! If you start out in even slightly the wrong direction you could add hours to your trek.

1

2

3

77

Get your bearing

1 First align the desired bearing on the dial with the direction of travel arrow.

2 Hold the compass in front of you and turn your body until the north end of the compass needle is directly over the orienting arrow.

head this way

Taking a bearing from a map

Your map does not have to be oriented to take a bearing. Place the compass on the map with the edge lined up against your desired line of travel. Rotate the dial until the "N" is aligned with the top of the map and the orienting lines are parallel with the north–south lines on the map. The bearing on the dial is the bearing you should follow.

Bypassing objects
You can also use bearings to make your way around obstacles.

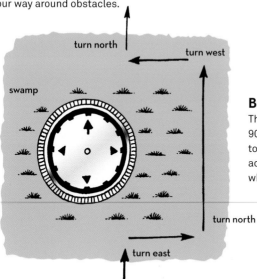

turn north

turn west

turn north

turn east

swamp

Basic bypass
This bypass involves three 90-degree turns with a fourth to bring you back on track. For accuracy, count your paces when bypassing.

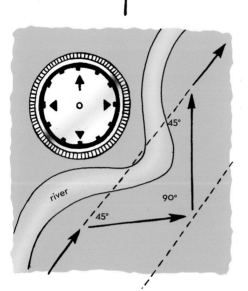

45°

90°

45°

45°

river

45- and 90-degree bypass
This bypass involves just three turns. Count your paces to ensure that each length is of equal distance.

Marker

Bypassing is easy if you can see a feature beyond the obstacle aligned with your bearing. In this case, walk around the lake until you reach the lone tree.

BEAR SAYS

Learning how to make bypasses to avoid dangerous obstacles can save precious time on a hike that could be spent setting up camp or preparing food.

Deliberate offset

Take a bearing left or right of your destination. That way, when you hit a "baseline", such as a road or river, you know which way to turn.

Other types of compass

Mirror sighting compass

This compass type is similar to an orienteering compass with the addition of a hinged mirror. This allows you to sight your target and your bearing at the same time.

mirror

dial

base

line of sight

BEAR SAYS

Trying out different compasses is not only useful, but fun too. Each has its own benefits.

Lensatic compass

In situations when an exact reading is required, a lensatic compass is best. They are the favoured compass type for military use. Many models have illuminated dial markings so they can be used at night.

cover

lens

base

line up slit with wire

wire

Thumb compass
These thumb-mounted compasses are used in orienteering.

Direct sighting
Look through the eyepiece to get a bearing accurate to within one degree.

Button
A compass doesn't have to be big to be useful. Keep a little one in reserve.

BEAR SAYS

Some mobile phones even come with a compass! You can't rely on the battery life though – so they aren't a replacement for proper kit.

Make your own compass

These are some simple ways to make your own magnetic device.

Magnetize

To make a compass, first magnetize a needle by stroking it in one direction with a magnet. If you stroke towards the point of your needle, the point will indicate north.

stroke direction

needle

insulated wire

Battery method

Alternatively, you can magnetize a needle by coiling some insulated wire around it. Connect the wire to a battery for five to ten minutes.

battery

mug

Now you know

If you gently lower the needle into a mug of water, surface tension should keep it floating (a coating of natural oil from your hair will help). The sharp end will point towards magnetic north.

GPS

Hand-held GPS units are a fantastic aid to navigation, and can be the difference between life and death in extreme survival conditions. However, they can't replace maps – you should always carry a compass and know how to use it in case your equipment fails.

The global positioning system

A GPS unit works by measuring its exact distance from a minimum of three satellites in space. The point at which the three signals intersect is shown with a black dot below. This point represents the position of the GPS unit on Earth.

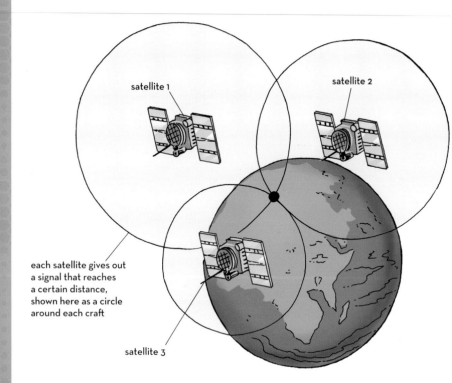

satellite 1

satellite 2

each satellite gives out a signal that reaches a certain distance, shown here as a circle around each craft

satellite 3

Go on a treasure hunt

If you like exploring, and have a GPS device, you can join the many hundreds of people who enjoy "geocaching". This hobby involves navigating to a set of coordinates and finding a container (the geocache) that has been hidden at that particular spot.

BEAR SAYS

There are 24 satellites in space that work together to make an accurate view of Earth.

Hand-held unit

A hand-held GPS unit will tell you your location, speed, and approximate altitude (height above sea or ground level). It will also permit you to retrace your path, guide you to specific waypoints or landmarks, and will work as a compass as long as you are moving in one direction. The more expensive models come with built-in maps, electronic compasses, and barometers (devices that measure pressure in the atmosphere).

display screen

buttons

OTHER WAYS TO NAVIGATE

Even without a compass it is possible to determine direction. The sun, moon, and stars can be signposts if you know how to read them. There are also lots of clues in the living world that can help you find your way.

Navigating the night sky

Looking up at the starry night sky is beautiful – and it can be useful too. The North and South Celestial Poles are the points in the night sky that appear to be directly overhead at all times. Finding these points can help you find the right directions. To find the north polar star (Polaris), first locate the pattern of stars known as the Plough or Big Dipper (Ursa Major). To find the south polar star, first find the constellation Crux.

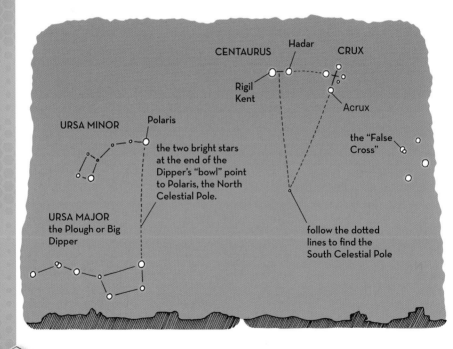

CENTAURUS
Hadar
CRUX
Rigil Kent
Acrux

URSA MINOR
Polaris

the "False Cross"

the two bright stars at the end of the Dipper's "bowl" point to Polaris, the North Celestial Pole.

URSA MAJOR
the Plough or Big Dipper

follow the dotted lines to find the South Celestial Pole

Lunar method

Imagine a line connecting the "horns" of the crescent Moon and project it to the horizon. This point indicates approximate south in the northern hemisphere or north in the southern hemisphere.

Watch method

Northern hemisphere
Point the hour hand at the Sun. Divide the angle between the hour hand and the 12 mark in half to find south.

Southern hemisphere
Point the 12 mark at the Sun. Divide the angle between the hour hand and the 12 mark in half to find north.

Shadow tip method

The shadow tip method works in either hemisphere and is most accurate around noon.

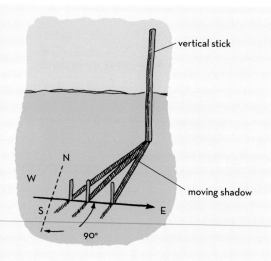

vertical stick

moving shadow

N

W

S

E

90°

1 Firstly, place a stick vertically in the ground. Mark the tip of the shadow made by the stick with a pebble or another stick.

2 Wait at least ten minutes before marking the shadow's tip with a second marker.

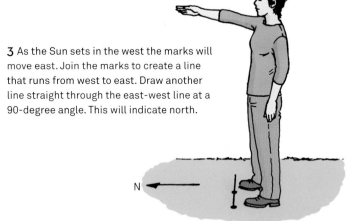

3 As the Sun sets in the west the marks will move east. Join the marks to create a line that runs from west to east. Draw another line straight through the east-west line at a 90-degree angle. This will indicate north.

N ←——

Compass-free map method

Align the features on a map with the corresponding features in the landscape. This will allow you to determine direction and work out your position.

BEAR SAYS

Using landmarks to pinpoint your location is something you can practise easily. Get a local map and go on a walk with a parent to give it a go.

point B on the map (a hill) lines up with point B in the landscape

point A (a church) on the map lines up with point A in the landscape

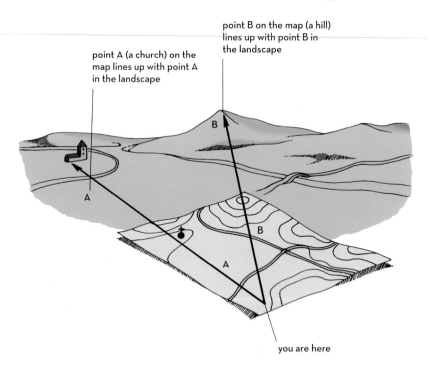

you are here

Night star method

This simple method uses stars to
pinpoint your location.

the string is a virtual
shadow of the star's light

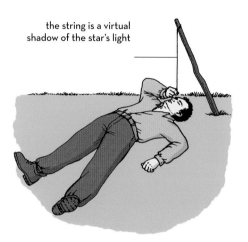

1 Set a long stick into the
ground at a slight angle. Tie
a length of string to the end
of the stick. Lie on your back,
place the string by your
temple, and align it with a
well-known star.

2 Mark the star's position on the ground
and then wait a while before marking it
for a second time. As with the shadow tip
method, the first mark will be west and
the second will be east.

mark the
position with
a stick

Signs in nature

Snow

Melted snow on one side of a tree will indicate south in the northern hemisphere.

Glacial boulders

These large rocks sit on pedestals of ice that erode on the south side in the northern hemisphere.

Green sign

Moss usually grows better on the shady side of a tree trunk – that's the north side in the northern hemisphere.

Magnetic termites

These Australian termites build their mounds aligned north–south to minimize exposure to the sun.

Traveller's palm

The leaves of this palm form a dramatic fan that is usually aligned east–west.

Nesting birds

If you are near water, look for signs of breeding wildlife, e.g. nests or frogspawn. Water birds, fish, and frogs often breed on the west side of a river or lake.

Prevailing wind

The most common wind direction that a location experiences is called the prevailing wind. The place the wind has come from brings different types of weather. The prevailing south-west wind in Britain, for example, is partly why it often rains more than other countries.

Spider webs

Do you know which way the wind tends to blow? Spiders do, and will orient their webs sideways to the prevailing wind.

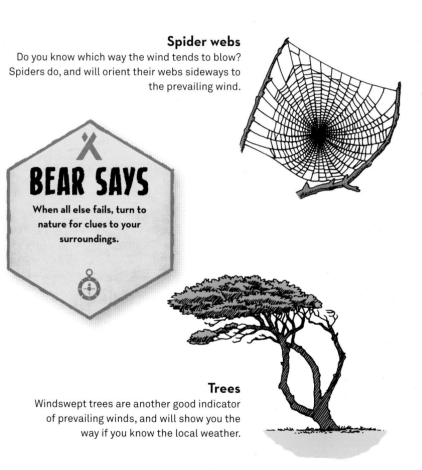

BEAR SAYS

When all else fails, turn to nature for clues to your surroundings.

Trees

Windswept trees are another good indicator of prevailing winds, and will show you the way if you know the local weather.

KNOTS

People have used the knots included in this book for years and they are just as valuable today. Early uses included making shelters, weaving, fishing, and tethering animals. Although they can take a while to master, the moment you tie a tricky knot and get to use it in action, you realize how exciting this ancient art can be!

IN THIS SECTION:

DISCOVER KNOTS!

A sound knowledge of ropes and knots is extremely important for climbers and mountaineers, but they also have uses in everyday life. It takes time and practice to master the art of knot tying, but it is very rewarding to put your skills to use!

Types of rope

Static ropes do not stretch, while dynamic ropes allow some movement if the load they are holding suddenly falls.

Laid rope

This rope is used in many outdoor activities. It has three or more strands twisted around each other.

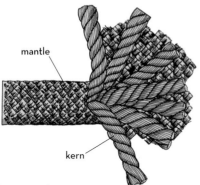

individual fibres make up each strand

mantle

kern

Kernmantle rope

Many climbing ropes have a protective sheath, called a mantle, covering the core fibres (kern).

Damaged ropes

The sheath of kernmantle ropes can hide a damaged core. Bulges in the core or tears in the mantle mean that the rope needs to be replaced.

damaged core

damaged mantle

Learn the terms

Turn	The U-shape that is formed when a rope is hung over a rail.
Round turn	A round turn is created when a rope is hung over a rail, and then wound around the rail one more time.
Half hitch	This knot is made when a rope is hung over a rail, then either under, or both under and over, itself.
Clove hitch	Two half hitches that are connected and placed next to each other make a clove hitch.
Standing end	The standing end, or standing part, refers to the main body of the rope.
Overhand turn	A circular shape in the rope where the working end finishes on top of the circle.
Underhand	A circular loop in the rope where the working end sits on the underside.
Working end	The portion of rope, other than the standing part, that is used to tie a knot. When the knot is finished, the working end is usually the small tail left over.
Bight	A bight is a U-shaped form made in the rope as part of the knot-tying process.

Carrying ropes

1 Put the two rope ends together. Measure out two armlengths, then loop the rest of the rope in double armlengths over your knee or around your shoulders. This is the main section that will sit on your back.

these two ends will become the shoulder straps

3 Pass a bight of rope through the top of the looped rope.

2 Wrap the two long ends tightly around the whole coil several times.

4 Run the loose ends through the bight of rope.

5 The whole rope should now hang neatly, with two long ends.

6 Run the long ends over your shoulders, then across your back, and tie across your stomach.

OVERHAND LOOP

One of the quickest ways to make a fixed loop in a rope is the overhand loop, suitable for a quick secure on a belay station. This knot can become very tight, however, and can be difficult to undo, so it isn't always the best choice.

Loop knots are closed bights that have been tied either in the bight itself, or at the end of the rope.

1 Put the two rope ends together. Stretch the loop out over the top of the trailing rope.

loop follows the direction of the arrow

trailing rope

2 Pull the loop through the hole.

3 Attach the loop to a carabiner (metal loop, with a spring-loaded opening).

BEAR SAYS

This knot is suitable for a quick secure on a belay station (the point on the rope from which a climber can hang and lower their partner down).

FIGURE-OF-EIGHT LOOP

Although a bulkier knot, this is thought to be one of the most secure ways to create a loop in a rope, and has many uses.

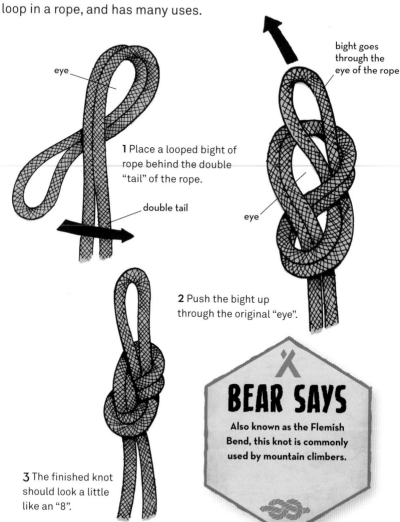

eye

1 Place a looped bight of rope behind the double "tail" of the rope.

double tail

bight goes through the eye of the rope

eye

2 Push the bight up through the original "eye".

3 The finished knot should look a little like an "8".

BEAR SAYS

Also known as the Flemish Bend, this knot is commonly used by mountain climbers.

THREADED FIGURE-OF-EIGHT

This should end up looking the same as the figure-of-eight loop knot, but it allows you to tie in to a fixed point, such as a harness or sling. It is done in two parts.

1 Start by tying a single, loose figure-of-eight knot in the rope, leaving a long tail. Thread the tail through the harness or sling, then start threading the rope back through the knot.

harness or sling

tail

2 The trick is to follow the original figure-of-eight knot, but backwards.

3 Make sure the rope follows exactly the same path as the original figure-of-eight and pull the tail through.

4 Again, at the finish it should look like a number "8".

JURY MAST KNOT

This knot can be used to "jury rig" (temporaily fix) a boat's mast if the existing rigging fails. The ropes holding the makeshift mast upright attach to the knot's three adjustable loops. A jury mast knot can also be used to put up a tent or flagpole, as long as there is something to prevent the knot sliding down.

1 Working from left to right, make three underhand turns. The left edges of the second and third turns should overlap the right edges of the first and second turns.

2 Lead the left hand into the first turn from underneath, over the left edge of the second turn, under the right edge of the first turn, and pick up the left edge of the third.

3 With the right hand, lead over the right edge of the third turn, under the right edge of the second turn, over the left edge of the third turn, and pick up the right edge of the first.

Centre of
second turn

4 Draw your hands apart far enough so that two loose bights begin to form. The remainder of the knot should be circular in shape with an obvious hole in the middle.

5 The second turn is still in the circular portion of the knot. Draw it out carefully at the top to form a third bight. Adjust the knot so that the three bights are of a similar size.

6 Place the knot over the end of a spar, and adjust to fit snugly. Tie both standing ends together around the spar. The three bights become attachment points for stays.

7 The stays – ropes or wires supporting the mast – can be attached to the jury mast knot with sheet bends or double sheet bends.

ANGLER'S LOOP

The angler's loop is a type of knot that forms a fixed, single loop, normally tied at the end of a rope. The angler's loop is difficult or impossible to untie, so it is best used where the line can be cut once the loop is no longer needed.

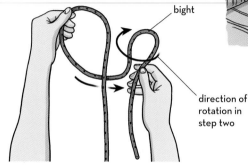

bight

direction of rotation in step two

1 Begin with a working part twice the length of the loop you wish to make. Make an underhand turn and then form a bight in the working end.

2 Rotate the bight right to left, then lead it through the turn from front to back. The bight will become the loop.

overhand
knot

the thumb
inserted
to show
channel the
working
end passes
through in
step 5

3 If the working end is too long, pull
the extra cord into the loop. Work it
out through the overhand knot and
into the standing end.

4 Lead the working end around behind
the standing part, next to the lower
portion of the overhand knot.

in shock cord, work slack out in stages
with fingers and tighten gradually.
Shock cord will tend to stretch rather
than slide through the knot

5 Slide the working end under both
strands of the loop, from right to left.

6 Tighten the knot by pulling on the loop,
the standing part, and the working end.
Pull hard on the loop and standing part
to complete, particularly in shock cord,
which stretches.

BOTTLE SLING

This knot provides a carry handle for a
bottle. It can be used to cool drinks in cold
water slung over the side of a boat. This
example requires about 1.5 m (5 ft) of cord.

Binding knots are tied
in a single piece of
rope, around bundles
of objects.

two
"ears"

centre of
original
bight

BEAR SAYS

The bottle sling was used by
ancient Greeks to carry jugs
and bottles and also to make
slings.

1 Fold the rope in half, and place the bight
flat on the table. Fold the bight down as
shown, to make two even sized "ears".

2 Slightly overlap the right ear over the
left. The centre of the original bight
should still be below the intersection
of the two ears.

3 Holding the pattern in place on the
table, draw the centre of the original
bight under the knot at the point of the
lower intersection of the ears.

draw the original
bight up through the
overlap of the ears

ensure there is
a hole for the
bottle neck here

4 Now bring the centre of the original bight up through the space formed by the overlapping ears, to make a new bight at the top.

5 Using both hands, turn the ears and centre part over at the same time, with the top moving away from you. The top of the ears now finish at the bottom of the pattern.

the ends can also be
tied to the bight to
form a handle or sling

6 Lift the knot carefully and place the hole over the neck of the bottle. Tighten by pulling on the upper bight and evenly on the pair of ends.

7 Work the knot to a snug fit around the neck of the bottle. The ends can be tied together to make a second handle, using a fisherman's knot or figure-of-eight bend.

ANCHOR BEND

The anchor bend, also known as the fisherman's bend, is quite a secure knot. It is most often finished by the addition of a half hitch. It will hold in bungee cord, whereas the "round turn and two half hitches" is particularly simple to tie, but it will not hold at all in bungee cord.

Bends are types of knots that join two separate pieces of rope.

1 Make a round turn through a ring, winding from back to front and left to right. Do not pull the turn tight yet, as the working end needs to pass through it first.

2 Lead the working end left behind the standing part, then to the front, and tuck it to the right beneath both windings of the round turn.

pull tight

3 Pull on both the standing part and working end to tighten the knot around the ring. This is a completed anchor bend, but a half hitch is usually added.

Round turn and two half hitches

round turn

first half hitch

1 Make a round turn through the ring as in step one. Pass the working end around behind the standing part, to the front, and under itself, to make the first half hitch. Pull tight.

with half hitch added

pull tight

4 Pass the working end around behind the standing part again, to the front, and under itself. Pull the working end as tight as possible.

pull each half hitch very tight

second half hitch added

2 Continue the working end in the same direction, around behind the standing part and to the front again, and make the second half hitch.

DOUBLE FISHERMAN'S KNOT

This is one of the best knots to safely tie two ropes together, and is useful on long descents. Start by laying the last metre of each rope alongside each other, tails in opposite directions.

1 Turn the end of one rope around the other rope twice, and pass the end back through the loops, away from the knot's centre. Do this to both ropes.

rope two

two turns

rope one

2 This should form two "x" shapes, which will then slide together as you pull each rope.

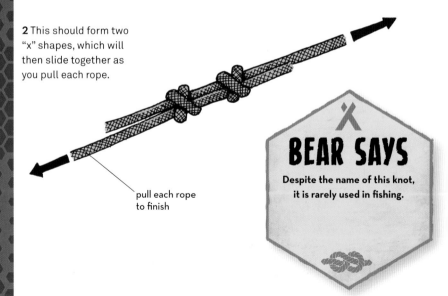

pull each rope to finish

BEAR SAYS

Despite the name of this knot, it is rarely used in fishing.

PRUSIK HITCH

The prusik knot is an excellent way to attach a weight to a rope. It slides up and down the rope when unweighted, but doesn't slip under a downward force. Two prusik knots (one for your feet, one clipped into the harness) are often used to climb up, or "prusik", a rope.

Hitches are used to attach load-bearing cordage to objects. The choice of hitch is important if the knot needs to remain secure.

1 Wrap the loop around the rope, and back through itself.

prusik cord must have a smaller diameter than the main rope

2 Repeat this process twice more so there is a triple loop top and bottom.

3 Push the knot together. It will slide up, but will hold if force is applied downwards.

CLOVE HITCHES

The clove hitch is a quick and memorable knot that can be used to attach a rope to a pole or a carabiner. It may slip on a smooth surface. The load can be applied to either end of the rope. Steps one and two show the clove hitch tied with a working end. The alternate "in-the-hand" method allows the hitch to be tied in the bight – anywhere along the rope.

1 Lead the working end over and down behind the pole, then up in front and over itself to the left.

2 Lead the working end diagonally across the turn, around the back of the rail again, then upwards under itself. You have formed two half hitches. Pull the ends to tighten.

Alternate clove hitch

This method can be used when you can slip the hitch over the end of a pole.

direction the loops will move in Step 4

left turn sitting over right

1 If you don't have easy access to the ends of the rope, tie the clove hitch using this alternate method. Begin by making two consecutive overhand turns.

2 Slide the left-hand turn over the right, then slide the fingers of the left hand through the centre of both loops.

3 When viewed from the side, the two half hitches can be identified. It is the same knot as shown in step two of the simpler clove hitch, shown to the left.

4 Simply slide the half hitches over the end of the pole and tighten.

Clove hitch for a carabiner

This hitch is also used in climbing. It can be used to safely lower climbing gear from a great height. It increases the amount of friction on the rope but also allows it to slip, so it can be used instead of a belay.

1 Make two loops in the rope, both in the same direction.

2 Place the lower loop over the higher loop, so that both tails of the rope are in the middle of the hitch.

lower loop

higher loop

both rope tails are in the hitch's centre

3 Clip a carabiner through the two loops. The hitch is surprisingly strong.

ITALIAN HITCH

This hitch can be used to safely lower climbing gear from a great height. It increases the amount of friction on the rope but also allows it to slip, so it can be used instead of a belay.

1 Grab the rope with two crossed hands, palms down.

cross hands

2 Uncross your hands but hold onto the rope, twisting it into two loops.

one tail is below, the other above

3 Pull the two loops together.

4 Clip the carabiner through the two loops.

downward pull

PILE HITCH

Pile hitches can be used to attach a dinghy to a post, or an anchor line to a bollard. They can be tied in the bight or at the end of a rope. The length of the working end required to tie the hitch will depend on the thickness of the post. To untie, ease some of the working end back into the hitch until there is enough slack to lift the bight off the top of the post.

BEAR SAYS

Make sure there isn't tension on the other end of the rope while tying this hitch.

1 Form a bight long enough to pass several times around the post. Hold the standing parts in one hand. With the other, wrap the bight around the post, underneath both standing parts.

bight

standing part

bight goes over the top of the post

2 Widen the bight and place it over the top of the post.

Double pile hitch
The double pile hitch is very secure but a little more complicated to untie.

1 Complete step one of the pile hitch (shown left), then wind the bight around the post a second time, before placing it over the post. The second winding is made lower down the post than the first.

3 Pull evenly on both ends to firm the hitch. If the rope is sticking and not tightening evenly around the post, you may have to help it, but be careful not to catch your fingers.

2 Adjust the hitch as in step three of the pile hitch. With both hitches, make sure that you hold the ends together until the bight is placed over the post, so that both ends are secure.

HIGHWAYMAN'S HITCH

The highwayman's hitch is a useful knot to know because it instantly releases with a tug on the working end. However, it is not the most secure of hitches can be loosened quite easily.

BEAR SAYS

The highwayman's hitch isn't secure enough for use in climbing or mountaineering.

first bight

standing part

leave a longish working end

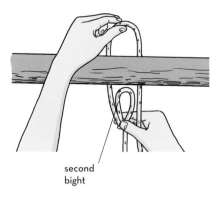

second bight

1 Form a long bight in the left hand, with the working end to the right of the standing part, and lead it up behind the rail.

2 With the right hand, form a second bight in the standing part, with the remainder of the standing part on the right side of this new bight.

second bight
led into first

working
end

standing
part

3 Tuck this second bight up through the first, hold it in place with your left hand, and tighten the first bight around the second by pulling on the working end.

third bight

working
end

4 With the right hand, form a third bight in the working part, with the working end to the right.

third bight led
into second

5 Lead this third bight fully up into the second, so that there is no slack around the rail.

pull on working
end to release

pull on
standing
part to
tighten

6 Pull on the standing part to firm the second bight around the third. To release, pull on the working end and the hitch will slide apart.

TIMBER HITCH

The timber hitch is an easy method of securing a rope to a pole. With the timber hitch tied at the centre of gravity, the pole can be hoisted up. The addition of a half hitch forms the killick hitch, which allows the pole to be towed on land or through water. The timber hitch is also used to attach nylon strings to a guitar bridge.

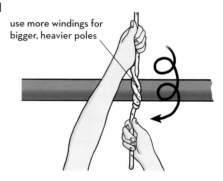

use more windings for bigger, heavier poles

2 Wind the working end around the turn again once, twice, or three times. Pull tight on the standing part and ease the slack out of the windings through the working end.

alternatively, go over the turn first, then under it from left to right

1 Make a loose turn around the pole from the back to the front. Pass the working end behind the standing part, to the front, and under the turn.

Killick hitch

add a half hitch some distance from the timber hitch

direction of pull for towing

3 Lead the standing part along the pole and tie a half hitch. Tying it nearer the end provides better stability when towing, but too near the end and it will slip off.

ROLLING HITCH

The rolling hitch is used to tie a rope to a pole or to larger rope, when the load is to be applied at an angle between 45 and 90 degrees to the pole. The direction of the load, or strain, will decide the way in which the knot must be tied. The hitches shown here take the strain from the right.

1 Begin the hitch with a round turn, going up and over, and from left to right.

2 Pass the working end diagonally left across both windings, then down around the back of the pole.

3 Tuck the working end up under the diagonal. Note that the rolling hitch is actually a clove hitch with an extra turn around the pole on the right.

BEAR SAYS

The tautline hitch is similar to the rolling hitch, and is suitable for attaching a line to a taut rope.

load the hitch
from the right

4 Pull both ends to tighten. The load can be applied from the right of the hitch. For loading from the left, begin tying the hitch as in step one, but winding from right to left.

5 Lead the working end up behind the rope, to the front, and tuck it under itself, parallel to the standing part. The knot looks like a cow hitch with an extra turn.

Tautline hitch

load the hitch
from the right

1 Tie this hitch using a line that is at least half the diameter of the taut rope. Complete step one of the rolling hitch, then lead the working end left in front of the standing part.

2 Pull both ends to firm the hitch tight around the rope. As with the rolling hitch, the strain can be applied from the direction in which the initial overhand turn was made.

TRUCKER'S HITCH

As it can be tensioned further after tightening, this knot is suitable for tying tent stays, or securing a load on a trailer. The hitch provides leverage, allowing the rope to be pulled tight, and uses up any excess cordage.

BEAR SAYS

The trucker's hitch is also known as the waggoner's hitch or dolly knot.

this knot requires a length of rope four to five times the distance from the hitch's starting point to the securing point

1 Begin with the standing part tied to an upper fastening point. Rotating counterclockwise, make a small overhand turn and secure it in your left hand.

2 With your right hand, form a bight in the working part. It will need to have a length approximately half the distance from the turn to the securing point.

shank

3 Lead the end of the bight into the overhand turn from below – not too far in, about a fifth of its length will do. Secure the bight and overhand turn in your left hand.

4 This forms a new, lower bight, called a shank. Lead the working end down and through the lower fastening point.

5 Lead the working end up through the shank from back to front. Apply downward tension to the working end. The turn will grip the bight and you can let go with the left hand.

6 Pull the end as tight as necessary and tie it off above the fastening point – a couple of half hitches should do. The trucker's hitch requires some practice to master.

SQUARE LASHING

Square lashing is a relatively easy way to secure two poles at right angles. Be careful with the tension and the number of windings – the lashing must be strong enough for the job, but not so tight that the poles are bent.

> Lashing is a method of fastening items together with cord. They are permanent and use multiple windings.

later additional windings will lock the tail securely.

BEAR SAYS

To join poles together, lashings are used. They can be useful around campsites to help build chairs and tables.

1 Tie a clove hitch to the vertical pole. Wind the tail and standing part together. Place the horizontal pole on top of the vertical. Lead the ends over both poles to the right.

path the end follows to form the first winding

2 Maintaining the tension, lead the cord behind the upper vertical pole, over and down in front of the left horizontal pole, around behind the lower vertical pole and to the front.

3 Repeat the winding process about four times. The number of windings will depend on the diameter of the poles and the thickness of the cord.

frapping turns do not bind pole to pole but compress the existing windings

4 Start the frapping turns. Make a turn over the right horizontal pole, then wind clockwise between the two poles three or four times.

clove hitch to finish

5 Stop at the top left and tie a tight clove hitch around the upper vertical pole, so the lashing can't slide or rotate under tension.

DIAGONAL LASHING

Diagonal lashing is used to secure poles that cross diagonally together. The two poles don't have to be at right angles – the timber hitch at the start pulls both poles together without changing their position. However, if the poles are not held in place, the angle can be difficult to keep during lashing.

the tension applied in the diagonal lashing process isn't as great as in square lashing, but there is less chance of the poles sliding

lead the cord away from you and around the back

1 Tie a timber hitch around both poles, at the intersection with the widest angle. Tighten the hitch and lead the cord away from you, around the back of both poles.

start lashing through the wider angle first

If the poles are fixed, wind the same number of times as for the wider angle

2 Wind tightly over the top of the hitch and around the middle four or five times. Unless the poles are fixed, the tighter you wind, the wider the angle becomes.

3 Now wind across the other, narrower angle. If the poles are not fixed, apply pressure and continue winding until you achieve the angle you want.

three or four frapping turns should do

tie off with a clove hitch

4 Wind the cord counterclockwise by passing in front of the upper vertical pole, behind the left cross pole, in front of the lower vertical pole and behind the right cross pole.

5 Finish with a clove hitch around one of the poles. Line it up with the end of the frapping turns so that there is little chance of the hitch sliding or rotating under tension.

SHEAR LASHING

A shear lashing can secure two poles together to reinforce them. It can also extend a pole if the lashing is placed near the end, at the point where the two poles overlap. Tied a little more loosely, it makes an A-frame lashing. Here, the two poles are separated slightly so that they can be moved apart. The A-frame is also known as shear legs and can be used for a tent or lean-to shelter.

cover the short end of the clove hitch with the lashing

1 Lay two poles side by side and tie together with a clove hitch. Leave the shorter end long enough to be secured underneath the windings.

2 Begin winding, but not as tightly for an A-frame as for securing two poles. As a rule, make the binding length no less than the width of the two poles.

cover the short end
of the clove hitch
with the lashing

3 For the frapping turns, lead the cord behind the top pole and to the front between the poles. Wind across the existing windings, between the poles.

4 Finish at the opposite end to the original clove hitch and tie another clove hitch around one pole, not both. The hitch must be tight, and snug against the lashing.

5 If tying poles together to reinforce or extend them, make a tighter binding, leave out the frapping turns, and finish with a clove hitch around both poles.

scissor action to
generate A-frame

6 To use as an A-frame, separate the poles by using a scissor action, stretching the cord equally at both ends of the lashing. Practice will help you apply the right lashing tension.

TRIPOD LASHING

There are different methods of tying tripod lashings but this one can be tied into a frame, taken to a site, and put up. After use it can be folded flat and taken away, with a temporary binding (such as the pole lashing) securing the other end. However, it doesn't form the perfect triangle shape at its base. Like the shear lashing, the angle at which the legs can be separated depends on the length and tension of the lashing, and the stretch in the cord.

when beginning, leave space for the width of the lashing plus enough space to hang an item

1 Lay three poles side by side, making sure the ends that will stand on the ground are even. Tie a clove hitch around the top pole at a suitable distance from the ends.

2 Wind the short clove hitch end around the working end and lead both ends towards you across the three poles. This will help lock the clove hitch and its tail.

3 Start winding between the poles: under the bottom pole, over the centre, under the top, then around and over, this time under the centre pole, and over the bottom.

wind for about the width of two poles. Stop with the cord coming from behind the top pole. Begin frapping turns

4 Begin frapping turns by leading the cord down in front of the top pole, then to the back between the top and centre poles. Form two or three turns around the windings.

5 Lead the cord behind the centre pole, and to the front between the centre and bottom poles. Make a second set of frapping turns in the opposite direction to the first.

6 To finish, tie off with a clove hitch around the bottom pole. The frapping turn must lead straight into the hitch so that there is no chance of it rotating.

7 To erect the tripod, separate the outer poles and use a scissor action to swing the centre pole in the opposite direction. This may be difficult if the lashing is too tight.

EYE SPLICE

Rope splicing is a way of joining two pieces of rope by unravelling their strands and then weaving them together. A splice is used where a rope is fixed permanently to an item or slipped over a hook, stake, or bollard. An eye splice isn't actually a knot, but a way to form an "eye" in the end of a length of laid rope.

Splicing is a traditional method used to permanently join two laid ropes.

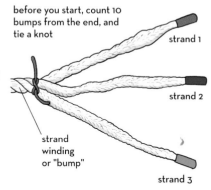

before you start, count 10 bumps from the end, and tie a knot

strand 1

strand 2

strand winding or "bump"

strand 3

1 Begin to unlay the rope. As you separate the strands, bind them with tape. Continue to unlay the strands up to the knot. Number each strand.

2 Open the lay of the rope to raise one strand. Feed the central strand, strand 2, diagonally left under the raised strand in the standing part. Do not pull it through completely yet.

next, tuck strand 3 through the eye

3 Feed strand 3, which is to the right of strand 2, under its corresponding right strand in the standing part, that is, the strand to the right of the one that strand 2 is tucked under.

strand 1 is the third to be tucked

begin the second set of tucks with strand 2

4 Rotate the rope slightly, and tuck the remaining strand 1 under its corresponding left strand of the standing part. Pull the three unlaid strands snugly up to the standing part.

5 Continue weaving the unlaid strands in this diagonal pattern until you have completed four sets of tucks. Three may be enough, but not if the lay of the rope is loose.

complete four sets of tucks

trim and seal ends

6 Maintain the even twist in the unlaid strands as you tuck. If you don't open the lay in the standing part sufficiently, the twist in the strands will increase as you go.

7 Thick rope may need the assistance of a fid (a cone-shaped tool) for opening the lay. After the fourth tuck, the ends can be trimmed and either sealed with heat or whipped (binded with twine).

SHORT SPLICE

This is a method of permanently joining two lengths of laid rope of a similar thickness. This method avoids the rope becoming thicker at the join.

rope ends aligned

strand winding or "bump"

1 Tie a constrictor knot around each piece of rope about 12 bumps from the end. Tape and number the strands and unwind them. Align the strands of the rope ends.

begin tucking the left rope into the right

2 Following steps two to four of the eye splice (p.41), begin to weave the left rope into the right. Make two sets of tucks.

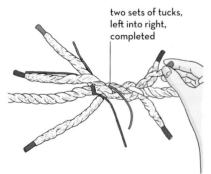

two sets of tucks, left into right, completed

3 Make a set of tucks of the right rope into the left. Tighten the strands and adjust the alignment of one rope to the other. Loosen the constrictor knots as needed.

one set of tucks,
right into left,
completed

four sets each
way completed

4 Make another set of tucks with the right rope into the left, so that there are two sets in each direction. Then make alternate sets until you have four in each direction.

5 The splice is completed and the ends can be trimmed and sealed. However, if you wish to taper the splice so that it blends neatly into the rest of the rope, proceed to step six.

taper
completed

6 An easy way to taper is to not tuck one strand of each set after three tucks, leave out a second strand after the fourth tuck, and make a fifth tuck with the one remaining strand.

7 When the tucking of each strand is completed in the correct order, the splice will have an even taper. Trim and seal the ends neatly.

IMPOSSIBLE KNOT

Put a length of rope in front of your friends and challenge them to pick it up then tie a knot without letting go with either hand. The result must be a proper knot that does not collapse when the rope is pulled tight.

BEAR SAYS

The trick behind mastering the impossible knot is plenty of practice, so you can demonstrate it quickly!

1 Lay the rope on a table. Before picking it up, cross your arms over each other. Now lean over and pick up one end of the rope in each hand.

Rope tricks are ways of tying and untying a knot that at first glance appear impossible!

2 Keeping a firm hold on the rope, uncross your arms and move your hands apart, letting the rope slip over your wrists and hands as you do so.

3 With this trick, you tie an overhand knot in the rope without letting go of either end.

RING DROP

This trick allows you to remove a ring that has been threaded onto a loop. The loop should be made from a length of thin cord about one metre (3 ft) long. Practise this first so you know how to do it quickly, then amaze your friends by getting them to try first – then if they can't figure it out, show them how it is done!

1 With the loop hanging over both your thumbs, hook the right little finger around the upper strand, to the left of the ring and from behind.

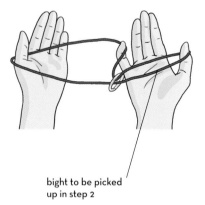

bight to be picked up in step 2

2 With your left little finger, reach over the bight formed by the right little finger, and hook it around the upper strand to the right of the ring, again from behind.

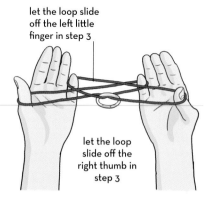

let the loop slide off the left little finger in step 3

let the loop slide off the right thumb in step 3

3 To free the ring, move your hands apart while letting the loop slip off the left little finger and the right thumb.

NOT A KNOT

This trick, which begins with a reef knot, looks very complicated, but the knot falls apart completely when pulled tight. The final step is easiest to carry out if thin cord or flexible rope is used rather than thick or stiff rope. A piece of cord about one metre (3 ft) long is ideal.

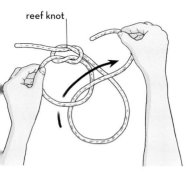

reef knot

1 Form a loop and tie a reef knot. Pick up the working end that emerges towards the back of the knot and lead it through the loop from back to front.

2 Lead the same working end through the centre of the reef knot, again from back to front.

BEAR SAYS

Once you have mastered the puzzle, give a reef knot to your friends and challenge them to make it collapse without untying it.

3 Pull firmly on both ends of the cord. The original reef knot will collapse and disappear completely.

DANGERS AND EMERGENCIES

There is so much out there in our amazing world to explore and experience, yet it is vital that you remain unharmed as you pursue new adventures. Our planet and its creatures can be dangerous at times, so learn the skills you need, and remain safe in the face of adversity.

Bear

IN THIS SECTION:

STAY SAFE IN THE WILD

When you set out on an adventure it is very important to be fully prepared in case you come into contact with danger. There are many ways to get help and avoid harm, so do your homework and stay safe.

Signalling for help

In an emergency your first contact with the outside world is likely to be a search aircraft. Make this contact count by learning standard ground-to-air signals. You can use objects, as well as your own body, to seek help.

raise one arm in the air

raise both arms in the air

All is well

Pick us up

hold both arms out

place both arms behind your head

hold out your right arm

Need mechanical help

Have radio

Can proceed shortly

lay down with both your arms above your head

Need medical help

raise both arms in the air and wave them

BEAR SAYS

If you are in distress, these signals could save your life. Choose a large, open area where you are most likely to be seen.

Do not attempt to land here

Land here

bend your knees and hold both arms out in front of you, pointing in the direction of landing

hold one arm out and wave it up and down

Use drop message

wave a piece of material from side to side

Negative (no)

wave a piece of material up and down

Affirmative (yes)

Fire cones
Keep these primed with plenty of dry fuel, and ready to go at all times.

Smoke cones
In the daytime, smoke marks your position more clearly than fire. Use fuel sources such as green branches and rubber.

BEAR SAYS
Wherever you are in the world, three objects together signal distress. Don't forget this international call for help!

Life rafts
In thick jungle, the only clear area may be a river. Tether together three rafts loaded with fuel for a jungle distress signal.

Smoke flare

flare smoke is usually red or orange and is designed to be seen up to 5 km away

end cap with pull cord firing mechanism inside

Other types of signals

strobe lights give out flashes of light to draw attention

LED flares give out light when an electric current flows through them

rocket flares can be seen up to 40 km away in good conditions

signal kite – these work best with a strobe light attached

rocket flare

Signal mirror

sunlight

mirror

aim with your fingers and reflect sunlight across them

signal mirror with sighting hole

A mirror is the most valuable means of signalling in daylight, as reflections can easily attract attention. Make sure to pack one if you are going off the beaten track.

Personal locator beacons

High-tech personal locator beacons (PLBs) are small, lightweight devices that can be used in an emergency anywhere in the world. First of all, the PLB is activated (1), then a signal is sent to a satellite network in space (2). A ground station then receives the signal relayed by a satellite (3). The search and rescue coordination centre is alerted (4) and then help is sent (5).

PLB

Aircraft signals

A rocking wing
If a plane rocks its wings the pilot has understood your signal.

Flying clockwise
This manoeuvre indicates that your signal is not understood.

Prepare a helicopter landing zone

helicopters land at an angle and need a clear approach, ideally downwind

mark the boundary of the landing zone with bright, weighed-down clothes or tarpaulins

clear an area of at least 18 m in diameter – the ground should be as flat as possible

stand outside the landing zone, but make sure you are easy to see

attach light fabric to a pole to show wind direction

DANGEROUS ANIMALS

Most creatures will avoid human contact, but it pays to know what species are dangerous and what your defences are.

Insects

Insects are small, often winged animals with six legs. Most are harmless, but some can be deadly.

Bee

A bee sting is painful but only life-threatening to those who are allergic. If you are attacked by a swarm of bees, run away from the point of first contact, protect your face, and seek shelter.

Ant

Ant stings range from harmless to agonizing. Be sure to avoid the bullet ant of Central and South America. Its sting is considered the most painful of any bee, wasp, or ant.

Wasps and hornets

Relatives of bees and ants, these insects can sting over and over. They can be aggressive when seeking food, and are drawn to sweet odours. Stay away from nests as allergic reactions can be fatal.

Mosquito

The mosquito is one of the deadliest creatures on Earth. Mosquito-borne diseases are a big problem in the tropics, but can occur in temperate regions too.

Flea

A flea bite is normally just an irritation, but they can lead to many diseases, including Lyme disease and even bubonic plague. It is sensible to consider them as a threat.

Tsetse flies

These large, blood-sucking insects are found in Africa between the Sahara and the Kalahari deserts. They carry the parasite that causes sleeping sickness, which can be fatal.

adult

larva

Botfly

An egg of the human botfly (native to Mexico, Central, and South America) hatches when it detects human warmth. The larva then burrows into the skin where it grows for about eight weeks. They may cause painful swellings but are otherwise harmless.

How to remove a botfly larva

1 The larva needs to breathe, so cut off its air supply by covering it with duct tape.

2 Apply pressure around the wound and grasp the larva tail with tweezers when it comes out.

3 Pull until the larva is completely out. Clean and bandage the wound.

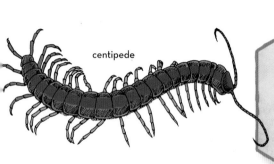
centipede

BEAR SAYS

Centipedes, especially the larger species, can inflict painful, venomous bites. If bitten, clean the wound and seek help.

Arachnids

Arachnids have eight legs and a body made up of two parts.
These are some of the most dangerous kinds.

BEAR SAYS

To remove a tick, use thin
tweezers, and grasp the tick as
close to the skin as possible.
Pull upwards with a steady,
even pressure.

Hard tick

These tiny bloodsucking
arachnids are responsible
for the spread of many
illnesses. The hard tick
family comprises the
majority of tick species.
They have a hard shield-
like plate just behind
their mouthparts.

Soft tick

The less common soft
ticks have a rounded,
leathery appearance with
mouthparts that can't be
seen from above. They
feed mostly on birds and
small mammals, but will
also choose human hosts.

Scorpion

About 25 species of scorpions can kill. They live in northern Africa, the Middle East,
India, Mexico, and parts of South America. Most of the other 1,000 or so species can
deliver a very painful sting.

Funnel-web spider

There are about 40 species of funnel-web spiders in Australia. The highly venomous Sydney funnel-web spider is possibly the world's most dangerous spider. It is likely to strike repeatedly if disturbed.

Widow spider

Many spiders in this animal group are highly venomous. Well-known species include the black widow (North America), the redback spider (Australia) and button spiders (southern Africa). Bites can be deadly.

Brazilian wandering spider

This group of aggressive spiders is found in Central and South America, and in banana shipments worldwide. Their venom is the most toxic of any spider.

Recluse spider

Bites from these spiders can cause cell tissue death requiring skin grafts and other surgery in extreme cases. Mild skin damage and itchiness is more common, however.

Tarantula

These frightening-looking spiders are actually quite timid. Most bites are similar to a wasp sting, although one species causes hallucinations. Some kinds shed irritating hairs as a form of defence.

Reptiles

Cold-blooded creatures, such as reptiles are covered with scales or bony plates. Snakes and lizards belong to this group – and many can deliver a potentially fatal bite.

American snakes

Copperhead

These well-camouflaged North American snakes will often freeze when feeling threatened. This means that bites often happen when they are stepped on by accident. Luckily, their bites are rarely fatal.

Rattlesnake
These snakes cause the majority of snake injuries and deaths in North America (even so, deaths are very rare). Despite their deadly reputation, rattlesnakes are timid, normally giving a warning rattle when alarmed.

Bushmaster
This genus of large venomous vipers is found in remote forested areas of Central and South America. The bushmaster is capable of repeated strikes and the injection of large amounts of venom.

Coral snake
There are over 65 recognized species of coral snakes in the Americas. They have very potent venom, but because of their mild nature and small fangs, deaths and injuries are rare. Many harmless snakes mimic the coral snakes' colouration for protection.

Cottonmouth
This viper is native to the south-eastern United States. A cottonmouth will vibrate its tail and throw its mouth open as a threat display. Bites are painful and can be fatal.

African and Asian snakes

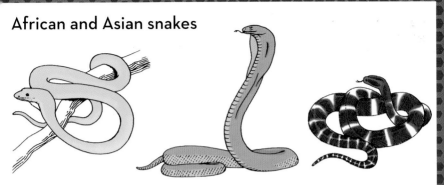

Boomslang
The venom of this sub-Saharan snake works as a hemotoxin – even small amounts will cause severe internal and external bleeding. They will strike fast if disturbed.

Cobra
Most cobra species rear up and spread their necks in a threat display. Some can "spit" venom up to 2.5 m (8 ft). They aim for their attacker's eyes. A direct hit causes severe burning pain.

Krait
This group of snakes is found in the jungles of India and Southeast Asia. They are armed with a neurotoxin that causes muscle paralysis (loss of movement).

Saw-scaled viper
These small snakes live in dry savannah habitats. They make a rasping sound when alarmed by rubbing the sides of their bodies together. They are very dangerous.

Puff adder
This snake species is responsible for more snake bite deaths in Africa than any other. When approached, it draws its head close to its coils, makes a loud hissing sound and is quick to strike.

Mamba
Most mamba species are tree-dwelling. The exception is the land-based black mamba – the world's fastest, and Africa's deadliest, snake. Untreated, its bite is fatal.

Australian snakes

Eastern brown snake
This snake species is responsible for most deaths caused by snakebite in Australia. Its venom is the most toxic of any land snake in the world, except for the inland taipan.

Red-bellied black
The red-bellied black is commonly found in woodlands, forests, swamplands, and urban areas of eastern Australia. They usually avoid attack. Bites are dangerous but rarely fatal.

Taipan
All species in this group are dangerous. The inland taipan is viewed as the most venomous land snake in the world. However, the human population of its habitat is low, and all bite victims have been successfully treated with antivenom.

Tiger snake
The common tiger snake is found in Southern and Eastern Australia. Their highly toxic venom is produced in large amounts. The venom mainly affects the central nervous system, but also causes muscle damage, and affects blood clotting.

Death adder
Death adders are found in most parts of Australia, New Guinea, and nearby islands. They have relatively large fangs and toxic venom. Before the introduction of antivenom, about 60 percent of bites to humans were fatal.

Sea snakes

Hydrophiinae
Found in warm coastal waters from the Indian Ocean to the Pacific, some species have venom more toxic than any land snake. Sea snakes are curious and will readily approach divers and swimmers, but they are generally placid and unlikely to attack.

European snakes

Adder
The common adder is the only poisonous snake of Northern Europe. It is widespread in highly populated areas, and bites are fairly common – but very rarely fatal. The common adder has several larger and more dangerous relatives in southern Europe.

BEAR SAYS

Snake venom can be deadly. It can contain neurotoxins that affect the body's nervous system, or hemotoxins that destroy red blood cells. Stay away!

Avoiding snakebites

Snakes are timid creatures. Unless they are stepped on, cornered, or handled, they present very little danger to humans. When you are in their habitat, follow these tips to avoid a bite.

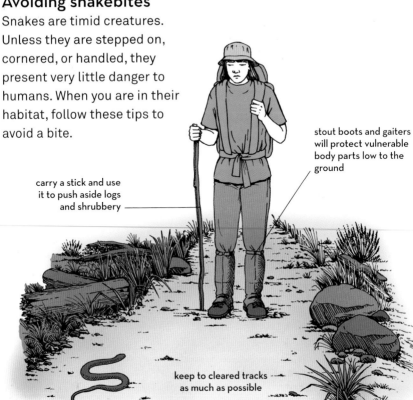

carry a stick and use it to push aside logs and shrubbery

stout boots and gaiters will protect vulnerable body parts low to the ground

keep to cleared tracks as much as possible

Treating snakebites

1 Snakebites usually occur on a limb. Start applying a pressure bandage just above the toes or fingers.

2 Continue as far up the limb as possible. This slows the movement of the venom and the onset of symptoms.

3 Apply a splint to the limb and keep it below the level of the heart. Keep the victim calm and make sure their breathing is regular.

Lizards

Gila monster

This venomous species is native to the south-western US and the north-western Mexican state of Sonora. Although a Gila bite is extremely painful, none has resulted in a confirmed human death.

BEAR SAYS

It is rare for a snake to actually chase a person, so if you come across one in the wild, stay calm and back away slowly.

Beaded lizard

A close relative of the Gila monster, the beaded lizard is found mostly in Mexico and southern Guatemala. Its bite causes terrible pain, swelling, and a rapid drop in blood pressure.

Crocodile

Two crocodile species – the Nile crocodile and the saltwater crocodile – are maneaters. Stay well away from water where they are known to be present.

Alligator

The American alligator is native to the south-eastern US. Alligators occasionally attack unprovoked, and their bites can cause dangerous infections.

quatic animals

Our oceans, rivers, and lakes can be deadly places. Knowing and recognizing these creatures is highly important if you are spending time near water.

Piranha

The mouths of these South American freshwater fish are packed with sharp triangular teeth that can puncture and rip. While they will not strip humans to the bone, piranhas will take bites of flesh and remove toes.

Candiru

The Amazon's most feared fish usually survives by invading the gills of larger fish, where it feeds on blood. However, it has also been known to lodge itself in the human urethra (the tube that connects the bladder to the outside of the body).

Bull shark

This shark species lives in both the open ocean and hundreds of miles up rivers. Because of their wide habitat range and aggression, many experts consider them the most dangerous shark species.

Electric eel

When angry, these large South American fish can deliver a burst of 600 volts – more than enough to kill. However, such deaths are very rare.

Flower urchin

Many sea urchins are armed with sharp spines and should be avoided. The spines of a flower urchin inject an extremely toxic venom. Injuries are very painful, and deaths have been reported.

Box jellyfish

These deadly jellyfish live in coastal waters off northern Australia and throughout the Indo-Pacific. A box jellyfish sting is so excruciating and overwhelming that a victim can go into shock and drown if swimming alone. Heart failure often follows.

Portuguese man-of-war

The sting of the Portuguese man-of-war causes severe pain and in some cases, fever and shock as well as heart and breathing problems. To treat, remove any stingers that are still attached, wash with seawater, then submerge the affected area in hot water.

Cone shell

These pretty marine snails use unique venoms to hunt their prey. A sting from a large cone shell brings severe pain and is potentially fatal. Treat as though it is a snakebite – there is no antivenom cure.

Blue-ringed octopus

These octopus live in tide pools in the Pacific Ocean from Japan to Australia. Although small and docile, they carry enough venom to kill 26 adults within minutes. Stings can bring total paralysis without loss of consciousness. Victims require artificial respiration for survival.

Needle fish

These shallow marine-dwelling fish make short jumps out of the water at speeds up to 65 km/h. Their sharp beaks can inflict deep wounds and often break off inside the victim.

Toadfish

Venomous toadfish dwell in tropical waters off the coasts of Central and South America. They have very sharp, very poisonous spines hidden in their dorsal fins. They bury themselves in the sand and are easily stepped on.

Stonefish

The world's most venomous fish, live in the coastal waters of the tropical Indo-Pacific. Symptoms of its venom are muscle weakness, temporary paralysis, and shock, which may cause death if not treated.

Shark

Although greatly feared, shark attacks on humans are extremely rare. No species is thought to target people as prey. Only a few kinds (the great white, tiger, and bull shark) have been involved in a significant number of fatal, unprovoked attacks.

Lionfish

This genus of aggressive fish is native to the tropical Indo-Pacific and has been introduced into the Atlantic coastal waters of the United States. Its venom can result in vomiting, fever, and sweating, and has been lethal in a few cases.

Stingray

These fish are mostly gentle, yet have a venomous barbed sting on the tail. People are usually stung accidentally when stepping on a stingray. Stings can result in pain, swelling, nausea, and muscle cramps.

Mammals

Mammals are warm-blooded animals that have fur or hair on their bodies, and they feed their babies with milk. Some large mammals, such as these, can be particularly threatening if disturbed.

American black bear

These medium-sized bears rarely attack humans but you should still avoid contact if possible. The most dangerous black bears are those that are hungry or have become used to human contact.

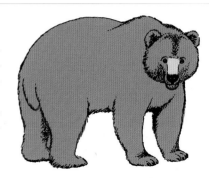

Brown bear

These large bears are normally unpredictable, and will attack if they are surprised or feel threatened. Mothers with cubs are particularly dangerous. If attacked, protect the back of the neck and play dead.

Polar bear

Contact with the world's largest land carnivore, or meat eater, should be avoided. A well-fed polar bear may show signs of curiosity near humans, while a hungry bear may stalk, kill, and eat you. Escape is unlikely without a weapon, but you could curl up and play dead.

Vampire bat

The common vampire bat is native to the American tropics and subtropics. They will feed on human blood when horse and cattle are in short supply. Their bites can cause rabies, a deadly viral infection.

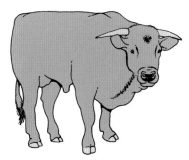

Bull

There is nothing like a large bull to turn a pleasant walk into a frightening ordeal. Never turn your back on a bull that has its head lowered or is pawing the ground. Back away slowly.

Rhinoceros

The five living species of rhinoceros are known for charging without being provoked. With very poor eyesight, they often panic at unusual smells and sounds.

BEAR SAYS

Never anger a hippopotamus! They are responsible for more human deaths in Africa than any other large animal.

Tiger

The tiger is the largest of the cat species. Human prey appears to be a last resort for tigers, but individual man-eaters have been responsible for hundreds of deaths.

Lion

As with tigers, humans are not a favoured prey of lions. However, where human settlements encroach on lion territory and regular prey animals are in short supply, lions will hunt and kill humans.

Leopard

Attacks by leopards on humans are rare, however injured, sick, or struggling individuals may turn to human flesh. The "Leopard of Panar" is reported to have killed as many as 400 people in northern India in the early years of the twentieth century.

Wolf

Like any large predator, a wolf is potentially dangerous, and common sense tells us to avoid them. Fortunately, attacks on people are very rare. Wolves with the disease rabies, in the "furious" stage, are the most dangerous.

DANGEROUS PLANTS

Plants have evolved a range of effective defences against animals that might want to eat them. Some need just the lightest touch and you're in trouble.

Stinging nettle

This plant is common in many temperate parts of the world. Hairs on the leaves and stems contain irritating chemicals, which are released when the plant comes into contact with skin.

stinging hairs

Cacti

Large cactus spines can be removed with tweezers. Work slowly because some spines have barbed ends. To remove very small, fine spines, apply duct tape to the area, then gently remove it.

poison sumac

Poison ivy, poison oak, and poison sumac

These plants grow in parts of the United States and southern Canada. People react differently if they come into contact with them, but most will be affected by rashes and blistering.

poison ivy

poison oak

Stinging trees

There are about 37 species of stinging trees across Southeast Asia, Australia, and the Pacific Islands. Avoid the Australian Gympie-Gympie, as one touch can mean months of agonizing pain.

QUICKSAND

Quicksand is a mass of fine sand, silt, and clay that has become completely saturated with water. While it's hard to get out of, it is possible to escape.

1 If you feel yourself sinking into quicksand, act fast.

2 Unstrap your pack or any other heavy gear and throw it aside.

3 Drop onto your back to spread your weight. Then, work to free your legs.

4 Use swimming or snake-like motions to return to solid ground. It may take hours to move a few feet, but you can take a break at any time.

BEAR SAYS

Escaping from quicksand is a battle. The number one rule is to keep calm. Once you have escaped, clean yourself off to prevent further harm from chafing.

SOURCING WATER

If you are lost or your supplies are running low, your first task should be to find water. In some places water is easily found, but in arid (very dry) areas it can be a life-or-death challenge.

Animal indicators

birds flying low and fast

many animal tracks leading downhill

ants moving upwards

Follow the animals

All living things need water to survive. Observe the animals in your surroundings and you will get valuable clues. Don't forget to look for plants. Unusually green plants in an arid landscape may indicate water just below the surface.

Ants in a row

A column of ants heading up a tree trunk may be heading to a reservoir of water.

Distance to water

Bees
Usually within 5 km.

Flies
Usually within 2.5 km.

Mosquitoes
Usually within 450 m.

Frogs
Usually in the immediate area.

BEAR SAYS

Don't give up too soon! You may need to dig down 1 m or more to reach water.

dig here

dig here

Dry riverbed

In a waterless landscape, a dry, sandy riverbed is often the best place to look for water. The best places to dig are the lowest points, the outside of bends, and near where green plants are growing.

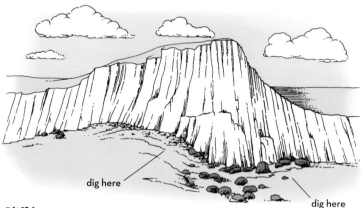

dig here

dig here

Cliff base

Water naturally pools at the base of cliffs and hills. Such pools are deep and often the last to disappear because they are protected or partially protected from the sun. If no water is found, dig in places where it would pool after rain.

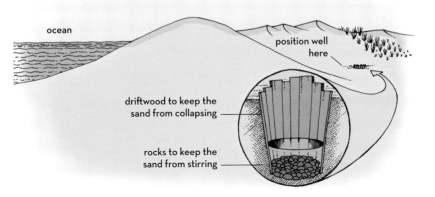

ocean

position well here

driftwood to keep the sand from collapsing

rocks to keep the sand from stirring

Beach

A beach well is just a hole, dug behind the very first sand dune in from the ocean. It should be about 1 m deep. Fresh groundwater seeping towards the ocean will gather in the well and float on top of the salty seawater.

timber shoring

stagnant, unsafe water

Seepage well

You may come across a stagnant body of water that is cloudy, has a bad flavour or odour, or is difficult to access. If this happens, dig a well about 10 m from the water source. The water that fills the well will be filtered and should be safe to drink.

WATER FROM PLANTS

If you can't find a water source in the environment around you, you can search for certain plants that can provide a drink.

machete

Mature coconut
Use a sharpened stake driven into the ground to split and remove the outer husk and reveal the shell. Drive a hole through a soft "eye" of the shell to access the coconut water.

Green coconut
Slice open a green coconut with a sharp knife to access the water inside. Drink the coconut water in moderation because it is a natural laxative.

stake

coconut husks

Banana tree
Cut through the trunk of a banana tree about 10 cm above the ground. Then, hollow out a bowl-like reservoir inside the stump. Water from the roots will gather in the bowl. Scoop the water out of the bowl three times before drinking as the water will be bitter at first.

carve bowl here

cut here

Green bamboo

Green bamboo can supply you with fresh water, even at the height of the tropical dry season. To collect water from a young stalk, bend it over, tie it securely, and cut off the top. Water will drip out of the cut. Collect it in a container.

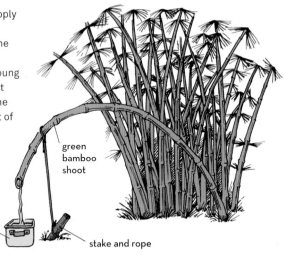

green bamboo shoot

collection container

stake and rope

make two 45° angle cuts

Big bamboo

For larger shoots of green bamboo, simply cut a hole near the base of each section and collect the water within.

Water from a vine

Cut a section of a vine high up. Then, sever it completely near the ground. Liquid will drain out the bottom. Don't drink from vines that produce white sap or milky liquid when cut. Get rid of liquid that has a sour or bitter taste.

Transpiration

This is one of the most efficient and easily constructed sources of water in an arid setting. Tie a plastic bag around a leafy branch of a medium-sized tree or shrub, and place a container underneath. After a few hours in the Sun, you will have some clean, drinkable water.

BEAR SAYS

Finding clean, safe water should always be your top priority. You can survive three weeks without eating, but only three days without water, so find it fast.

earth or rocks to weigh down the plastic sheet

drinking tube

foliage

collection container

Solar still

This system extracts water from the soil and any plants growing in or placed in a hole. Moisture evaporates, rises, and then condenses on the underside of the plastic barrier above, which then drips into a collection container below.

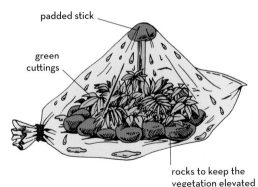

Water from cuttings

Collect as many green leaves and branches as can fit in a plastic bag without touching the sides. Prop up the centre to form a tent. Arrange the bag on a slight slope so the condensation will run down to a collection point.

padded stick

green cuttings

rocks to keep the vegetation elevated

prop up or suspend the top of the bag

grass or low shrub

collection channel

Ground transpiration

This arrangement works on the same principle as the transpiration bag opposite, but with plants that grow close to the ground. Consider scaling up from a plastic bag by using the fly of a tent.

prickly pear

Cacti

Cacti are a valuable survival resource in many deserts. The fruits of the prickly pear and some other species are edible. Many cacti contain huge amounts of water in their flesh that can be gathered in solar stills or transpiration bags. Cacti are protected in some areas and should only be used in an emergency.

saguaro

WATER PURIFICATION

In the wild, even water that looks pure and pristine may not be. Luckily, having clean drinking water is relatively simple when you have the right equipment and knowledge.

boiling vessel

condensation vessel

Distill
This system is trickier than simple boiling, but it makes drinkable water from sources heavy with sediment. It can also be used to distill seawater or urine.

Boil
This kills most types of disease-causing organisms. Boil the water for at least one minute, then let it cool down.

Chemical
Iodine, potassium permanganate, and chlorine can be used to treat water. They take time to work, and be prepared for a slightly odd taste.

Solar
Pour suspect water into clear plastic bottles and expose them to direct sunlight for at least six hours (or for two days in very cloudy conditions).

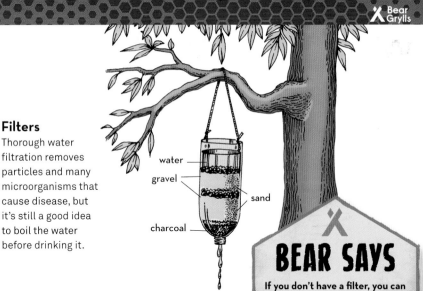

Filters

Thorough water filtration removes particles and many microorganisms that cause disease, but it's still a good idea to boil the water before drinking it.

water
gravel
sand
charcoal

BEAR SAYS

If you don't have a filter, you can make one using a plastic bottle, gravel, sand, and charcoal. The charcoal helps to filter out tiny impurities in the water.

virus and bacteria filter
parasite filter
carbon filter

Bottle filter

This filter bottle works with a cartridge that needs to be replaced after every 160 refills, or 216 gallons of water. Simply squeeze to produce a flow of water.

UV light emitter

pump handle

activated carbon

Pump filter

There are many pump filtration systems that hikers can use. Each stroke of the pump draws water through the filter and purifies it.

Ultraviolet

This battery-driven device uses UV light to sterilize 975 ml of water in 90 seconds. The water must be clear for the sterilization to work well.

FOOD FROM PLANTS

So you're stuck in the wilderness, and you've got plenty of safe drinking water. Your next priorities will probably be food and shelter. Plants can provide great nutrition if you know what's safe to eat.

Edibility test

1 Crush and smell the plant sample. Reject it if you sense strong, acid, or almond odours.

2 Crush and rub the sample against the inside of your elbow. Wait 15 minutes and discard if there is any irritation.

3 Hold a small amount against your lips. Reject if there is any irritation.

4 Place a small amount on the tongue. If there is any bad taste or irritation, throw it away.

5 Chew a small amount for several minutes, but do not swallow. If there is any irritation, spit it out.

6 If the plant part passes all these tests, eat a small amount and wait several hours for any adverse reaction.

BEAR SAYS

Tap along a piece of bamboo and listen to the noise it makes. Sections that have water inside will make a denser sound.

Split
Separate the plant into its basic components and test separately.

flowers

leaves

stems

roots

Plants to avoid

Some plants should be avoided altogether. Look for these indicators and leave them alone.

plants with seed pods

plants with milky sap

umbrella-shaped flower clusters

plants with shiny leaves

mushroom and toadstools – unless you are absolutely sure it is a safe species

Plants to eat?

Most foods eaten by primates and birds are safe for us to eat, too. But this is not a guarantee – always use the edibility test opposite. Many berries are safe to eat, but only take a bite if you are certain they are edible, such as blackberries.

HUNTING SMALL ANIMALS

In a survival situation, a meal of meat goes a lot further than plants alone. While large animals can be difficult and dangerous to hunt, their smaller relatives are easier to get onto your plate.

Hand weapons
These are some tools traditionally used to catch small animals.

throwing stick

weighted club

rock

slingshot

bola

rodent skewer

BEAR SAYS

Insects, frogs, lizards, and snakes are a good source of protein. Keep tiredness at bay with these energy sources in an emergency.

use this hand to grab the frog

keep this hand in positon

Catch a frog

Hold one hand about 50 cm (1.5 ft) in front of the frog and slowly wriggle your fingers. This will grab the frog's attention. Grasp the frog from behind with your other hand.

stout stick

Catch a lizard

Gently wave a noose of tight wire in front of the lizard. Gradually bring the noose closer and closer, then lasso the lizard.

forked stick

Catch a snake

All snakes can be eaten. To catch a snake, first stun it with a rock or stick. Pin its head down with a forked stick, and kill it with a knife, rock, or another stick. Cut the head off and bury it if there is any chance that it might be a venomous species.

Snares

These traps are used to catch some animals, often using wire or cord.

Simple loop snare

Make a snare about the size of your fist for small animals, such as rabbits. Set up about 15 snares for each animal you hope to catch.

wire snare

supporting twigs

Spring snare

Game running through a spring snare releases the trigger bar and is flung off the ground. It's useful for catching rabbits, foxes, and similar animals.

sapling

trigger

upright

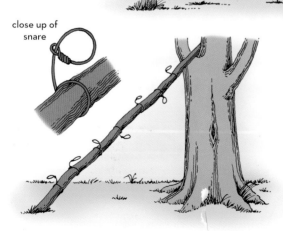

close up of snare

Squirrel pole

A squirrel pole is a long pole placed against a tree. Place several wire nooses along the top and sides of the pole so that a squirrel trying to go up or down the pole will have to pass through one or more.

Trapeze spring snare
This trap has two separate snares built into one mechanism. This will double your chances, or allow you to cover more area on a game trail.

springy sapling above

snare bar

BEAR SAYS

In my experience it is always best to set as many traps as possible so that you have a greater chance of catching a meal.

Figure-4 deadfall trap
This simple trap can be made to any size. A horizontal bait bar is balanced at right angles to an upright with a lock bar, which supports a rock or other heavy weight.

heavy log

bait

Deadfall trap
It's easy to build a deadfall trap large enough to kill a pig or deer. Make sure everyone in the party knows exactly where such a trap has been set as it could also harm a person.

heavy log

retaining bar

trip line

EDIBLE INVERTEBRATES

Insects, molluscs, and arachnids can be found in large quantities and they are highly nutritious. If survival is at stake, put your taste buds aside and add some of these critters to the menu.

Worms

There are few better sources of protein than worms. Drop them in drinkable water after collection and they will naturally wash themselves out. If you prefer, dry and grind the worms and add them to soup.

Snails

Starve snails for a few days so they can expel any poisonous plants they have eaten. Boil them for three minutes then drain, rinse in cold water, and remove from their shells. Avoid species with brightly coloured shells.

Spiders

Don't overlook spiders as a source of protein. Eat the bodies and leave the heads, which may contain poison. If you catch a tarantula, try frying it – they are a delicacy in parts of Southeast Asia.

Slugs

Some slugs are very large – three or four will constitute a good meal. They can be eaten raw, but are much more appetizing cooked. Prepare and cook them exactly the same way as snails.

Grubs

Insect larvae, also known as grubs, are prime wilderness food. They favour cool, damp places, so look in rotten logs, under the bark of dead trees, under rocks, and in the ground. Grubs are safe to eat raw.

Grasshoppers

These insects can be a great source of food in some places. Knock them from the air with a piece of clothing or a leafy branch. Remove the wings, antennae, and legs before eating them. It is best to roast them to kill off any parasites.

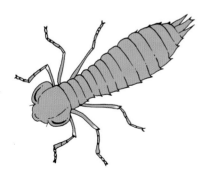

Termites

These insects exist in enormous numbers in the warmer parts of the world and are easily collected from their nests. Remove the wings from larger species before eating. They can be cooked, but are more nutritious eaten raw.

Aquatic insects

Nearly all water-based insects can be eaten in both adult and larval form. Use clothing as a net and trawl freshwater rivers or ponds.

EMERGENCY SHELTERS

Hot or cold, wet or dry, a good shelter is vital for your safety. Each landscape requires different types of shelter. Use the natural resources at hand depending on your need.

Desert shelter
Dig a hollow and cover with two tarpaulins one above the other.

insulation

entrance

All-natural shelter
A leafy bed, brush-covered lean-to, and a fire can keep you warm and dry.

Bough bed
A bough bed is made from evergreen branches arranged in overlapping rows. It will provide insulation, comfort, and will keep you above any rain that is running along the ground.

logs to keep the boughs in place

Fallen tree shelter

A fallen tree can make a quick shelter. Improve it by removing branches on the underside and slinging a tarpaulin on top.

check that the broken part is strong enough to last the night

tie the tops together

Sapling shelter

If you come across a group of saplings, clear the ground between them, strip their branches, and tie their tops together. Cover with material or weave branches between them.

hold up the "roof" with extra branches

weigh down the covering

BEAR SAYS

In harsh weather or desperate situations, shelters such as these can save your life!

Tree pit snow shelter

In forests where heavy snow has fallen, you will often find deep hollows under the branches of evergreen trees. Dig out some extra room if needed, and lay branches on the ground.

GLOSSARY

Analogue – An analogue device usually has a needle or pointer (think about clocks) and can show a continuously variable number.

Bearing – A bearing is the angle measured between north and an actual object.

Bight – A loop of rope.

Bypass – A bypass is an alternative route around an object.

Carabiner – A metal link with a safety closure, used by climbers to attach ropes, harnesses, and anchors.

Carbon monoxide – A colourless, odourless, toxic gas.

Chafing – When something irritates skin by rubbing against it.

Compass – An instrument used for finding your way, often alongside a map.

Concave – Curving in or hollowed inward.

Condensation – The process where a gas turns into a liquid.

Constellation – A group of stars.

Contour – A line that shows the 3D shape of something.

Convex – A convex shape is curved or rounded outwards.

Coordinates – A system that means every location on Earth can be described by a set of numbers.

Digital – A digital device usually has a computerized display.

Dynamic – Moving, not static.

Evaporation – The process where a liquid turns into a gas.

Flare – A very bright light that is used to send a signal, often used when signalling for rescue or to show your position.

Gully – A ravine formed by water.

Hitch – A dynamic knot that can be easily adjusted.

Horizontal – A line running from left to right.

Ignote – To set alight.

Insulate – To trap heat.

Kilometre – A unit of length equal to one thousand metres.

Landmark – An object that is easily seen from a distance.

Latitude – A position between North and South.

Latrine – An outdoor toilet.

Laxative – A food or medicine that causes you to poo.

Lensatic – A compass with a magnifying lens.

Longitude – A position between East and West.

Machete – A sharp knife used for chopping away plants in the wild.

Meridian – A circle of constant longitude around the world.

Orienteering – A sport involving navigational skills using a map and compass.

Paralysis – A condition that leaves you unable to move part or all of you body.

Prevailing wind – The most frequent wind direction experienced at a particular location.

Rabies – A disease that causes madness and aggression, transmitted through saliva and common in dogs.

Scale – The relationship between the distance on a map to the corresponding distance on the ground.

Stagnant – When unmoving water develops an unpleasant smell as a result.

Symbol – A picture, word, or abbreviation on a map.

Tarpaulin – Heavy waterproof cloth, often used for shelters.

Thermal – Relating to heat.

Temperate – An area with a mild climate.

Termite – An insect that usually lives in a large group.

Topographical – A topographical map shows the shape of the ground (e.g. flat or hilly) using contour lines.

Transpiration – The process where plants absorb water from the soil through their roots, and releases it through their leaves.

Tropical – An area of regular sun.

Urethra – The tube that connects the bladder to the outside of the body.

Venom – A dangerous toxin transferred via a bite.

Vertical – A line running from top to bottom.

Discover more amazing books in the Bear Grylls series:

Perfect for young adventurers, the *Ultimate Survival Handbook* accompanies an exciting range of colouring and activity books. Curious kids can also learn tips and tricks for almost any extreme situation in *Survival Camp*, explore Earth in *Extreme Planet*, and discover some of history's greatest explorers in the *Epic Adventures* series.

Conceived by Weldon Owen in partnership
with Bear Grylls Ventures

Produced by Weldon Owen, an imprint of Kings Road Publishing
Suite 3.08 The Plaza, 535 Kings Road,
London SW10 0SZ, UK

WELDON OWEN
Editor Susie Rae
Designer Shahid Mahmood
Contributor Jen Green
Illustrators Peter Bull Studios (original illustrations),
Bernard Chau (colours)

Printed in Malaysia
2 4 6 8 10 9 7 5 3 1

Disclaimer
Weldon Owen and Bear Grylls take pride in doing our best to get the facts right in putting together the information in this book, but occasionally something slips past our beady eyes. Therefore we make no warranties about the accuracy or completeness of the information in the book and to the maximum extent permitted, we disclaim all liability. Wherever possible, we will endeavour to correct any errors of fact at reprint.

Kids – if you want to try any of the activities in this book, please ask your parents first! Parents – all outdoor activities carry some degree of risk and we recommend that anyone participating in these activities be aware of the risks involved and seek professional instruction and guidance. None of the health/medical information in this book is intended as a substitute for professional medical advice; always seek the advice of a qualified practitioner.

A WELDON OWEN PRODUCTION. AN IMPRINT OF KINGS ROAD PUBLISHING.
PART OF THE BONNIER PUBLISHING GROUP.